A HISTORY OF POLITICAL IDEAS

A HISTORY OF POLITICAL IDEAS

By

C. R. MORRIS, M.A.
FELLOW AND TUTOR OF BALLIOL COLLEGE, OXFORD

AND

MARY MORRIS, B.A.
FORMERLY SCHOLAR OF SOMERVILLE COLLEGE, OXFORD

LONDON
CHRISTOPHERS
22 BERNERS STREET, W. 1

First published June, 1924.
Reprinted (revised) Dec., 1924.

CONTENTS

The Authors wish to express their gratitude to the Delegates of the Oxford University Press and to the Trustees of the Jowett Copyright Fund for kindly allowing them to include quotations from Jowett's translations of Thucydides and of Aristotle's *Politics*; also to Professor A. D. Lindsay for permission to quote from his translation of Plato's *Republic*, and for suggestions and encouragement throughout their work.

INTRODUCTION

A HISTORY of Political Ideas is calculated to be the butt both of the historian and of the philosopher. For what can be less historical than a discussion of the ideas in men's minds, what less philosophical than an arbitrary linking up of such ideas, merely because they follow one another in time ? It would be well to disarm such criticism at the outset by the frank admission that this book claims to be in the strict sense neither purely historical nor purely philosophical. Rather it attempts to examine the basis of certain political ideas which are commonly recognised to have had their influence on history, and, while taking that influence for granted, to attempt to estimate the permanent contribution which those ideas have offered toward the advancement of human political wisdom. So, though the selection of reformers and thinkers has been so far arbitrary that it cannot claim in any sense to cover, or even adequately to represent, the whole field of political philosophy, yet their thought has been treated in such a way that a certain historical and logical development emerges almost in spite of itself, and links up the separate stages of growth.

It is the nature of the subject itself that enables

one to recognise both that there is an essential like-
ness between, for instance, the political theories of
the fourth century B.C. and those of the present day,
and yet that in the intervening age the world has
been steadily advancing in a logical development
which is both registered in and influenced by the
theories of the centuries between. If we thus admit
that there is a fundamental sameness in human
nature which makes of history a continuous growth
whose thread can be dropped and picked up again
at will, we shall be less likely to be shocked by a
method which does not attempt to do more than consider the conditions of political life and thought at
certain particular stages. At each stage in turn we
shall be able to look both before and behind, to take
stock of the position that has been reached, and to
estimate its importance in the development of the
human spirit.

Little attempt has been made in this book to estimate or to work out the actual influence upon history
of the various philosophers and theories examined ;
it is rather concerned to attempt to discover what is
the truth underlying the theories which has enabled
them to exert that influence. In the study of
political organisation the student seems to be,
above all, dependent upon the past experience of
mankind, and it would seem, therefore, that no
sound theory of political society can afford to neglect
the lessons that are to be learned from an exami-

nation of the critical steps in the progress of human development.

One virtue of the Greek thinkers lies in the fact that they were enabled to see the problem simply and to see it whole. Their city states were so small and their organisation so simple that they could fall within the easy comprehension of every citizen. The simplicity of their institutions made it possible for Greek philosophers to attack fundamental problems confidently in a simple and direct manner ; thus it was a comparatively common phenomenon in Greek political life for a reformer to bring forward, not some particular reform on a matter of detail, but a completely new constitution—that is to say, boldly to make a fresh attempt to solve the problem as a whole on quite new principles. This does not seem to have meant that the Greeks over-simplified the issues, but rather that their states were so small and their administrative method so direct, that there was little chance for the theorist to lose himself in irrelevant detail. So it was that in their different ways Plato and Aristotle were able to give a clearer and more complete account of the nature of civil society than any subsequent thinker has achieved. The Greek was happy in his position ; for he could look upon the problem as essentially manageable, and could proceed with serene confidence to solve it by the unaided light of pure reason alone. From one point of view, then, it was bound to appear that all subsequent thinkers could only cover again in a detail-ridden and laborious manner the ground which had already been so brightly illuminated by the pure speculative reason of the Greek philosophers.

The Romans, like all the peoples of the world since their time, were less happily situated. It is clear that the fundamental difficulties involved in the organisation of a world Empire would not lend themselves to discussion and solution in the market-place as readily as the problems of government of the city state. The time had come when problems were so complicated that important political steps were bound to be taken more or less blindly, and only taken at all to avoid some imminent catastrophe. Statesmen were perpetually finding the difficulties left unsolved by the preceding age pressing upon them so urgently that they could only advance slowly, a step here and a step there, more in hope than in wisdom. So they patched up from time to time the principles they had inherited from their forefathers, and managed more or less successfully to keep out the insistent weather. So through the Middle Ages men patched and patched the principles of government they had received from Rome until they saw in what direction the great system which they were building was tending. Machiavelli showed it to them in its true light, and then at last they repudiated and destroyed it.

Then in the new world, Rousseau tried to establish

a new order by the pure intelligence alone ; but by now political development had proceeded too far, and pure reason unaided was helpless. The doctrines of Montesquieu, who, in his admiration of England, did not neglect the lessons to be learned from experience, were more fruitful ; guided by his writings, the American reformers founded that " rigid constitution" under which the United States are governed to-day. But the French Revolution has shown that the attempt to frame by pure thinking a working system of political institutions for the modern nation State is beyond the power of the human mind. Man has so much widened his conception of liberty and has so greatly increased his demands on the reasonableness and sensitiveness of the State, that, if we may so put it, the State can only learn to satisfy these demands by long experience and by persistent attempts to accustom itself to meet approaching troubles ; it is only by acquainting itself with the temper of its people that it can establish within itself a system of government which will bend and not break in the storm.

The business of the political theorist to-day would seem to be to watch the development of this State, and to learn the lessons of this development. Nor must he think that by so doing he is shirking the real problem ; he need have no fear that, while learning a great deal of political practice, he is advancing not a whit in political theory, or that, while he is becoming learned in knowledge of what is, he is still no better prepared for making up his mind what ought to be. In politics it is impossible to separate the examination of what is right from the analysis of what is possible. No doubt Plato would have thought that democracy was good, could he have thought it possible. The development of the State, like growth in organic life, often brings forth better things than we could have dreamed of ; we have then to widen our scale of values to include such new experience. So while we, like the Greeks, approached our enquiry confidently assured that pure reason would triumph, we lay it down in a far different spirit ; for we are forced to recognise that the theorist must always wait upon the vote of the plain man, and that the issue of the struggle between the State and rival associations lies even in theory, as it clearly does in practice, beyond our telling.

A HISTORY OF POLITICAL IDEAS

CHAPTER I

THE GREEKS : THE *REPUBLIC* OF PLATO

WHEN the Greek looked upon the world he saw that it was intelligible, and that it was man's most natural pursuit and his most obvious duty to try to understand it. When he thought about the " good life," it appeared to him that there must be on all occasions one thing which it is right to do, one course which it is right to pursue, and that it was man's business to find this right course and pursue it. So also in political life there was for the Greek always one policy which was the best policy, one constitution which was the best constitution, and all that was necessary was to discover that policy and to follow it, to find that constitution, and to preserve it.

To this essentially simple view it might be objected that some things are, as we say, a matter of opinion ; that Themistocles might advise one thing, Aristides another, and there might appear to be " nothing to choose " between the two views. It might seem that whenever we act we do and must act on the strength of opinion only, and that our action can never be based on certain knowledge ; we can never know all

1

the facts, so that all we can do is to discover all that we can, and then make up our minds and act on our decision. Further, it might be claimed that this is what is of importance morally ; our actions are good, not if we do what is in fact the right thing to do, but if we do what we honestly think to be right.

Now the Greeks sometimes, no doubt, thought of things in this way, but it was not natural to them. It seemed to them less important that things were a matter of opinion than that one opinion was always better than another, in that it was nearer the truth. There must, therefore, be a truth, and knowledge of that truth will be better than any opinion ; moreover, the mind of man is equipped to find this truth. It should therefore be man's purpose, they thought, to find it once and for all, so as to be able to live their lives always in the light of it. Pythagoras and his followers had taught that in mathematical studies it was possible to arrive at certain knowledge ; in that sphere there was no place for mere opinion, since every proposition could be finally proved—a wrong view could always in the end be proved to be wrong, and the truth could be proved to be true. So the conclusion was drawn that not only mathematics, but everything in the world could be explained and understood in a similar way, if only things were examined from the right angle.

How, then, was the truth to be discovered ? Clearly, as in mathematics, it must be by thinking ; for it is the thinking mind which alone can win its way to understanding and knowledge. The political thinker then must follow the example of the mathematician ; all he has to do, thought the Greeks, is to collect his evidence and sift it and thus he will discover the truth ; so he will find the one ordained solution to the political problem, just as the student finds the one right answer to any arithmetical sum. Thus it seemed that the solution of the problems of political life, like the solution of all other problems, depended simply on knowledge.   Knowledge was the one thing which was worth following and preserving in whatever sphere of life.   So the Greek ideal State was a commonwealth organised and governed with the greatest wisdom ; and since the greatest wisdom would seem to reside in the ideally wise man, the central point in Greek political philosophy is the doctrine of the Philosopher King.   In practice, of course, they recognised that an ideally wise man was unobtainable, and they preferred, therefore, to put their trust in other forms of government.   Yet it would seem that, in spite of this, they all thought in their hearts that government by the wisest man was really the ideal.

It is this insistence on the importance of wisdom which explains the curious paradox underlying Greek political thought.   The Greeks saw as clearly as any people that the end of the State was an ethical end— that the business of political society was to make possible and to promote the good life.   Yet their ideal for civil society involved a form of government which, to modern eyes at least, renders impossible a truly ethical life for individual citizens, since all must submit themselves unconditionally to the commands of an absolute ruler.

Yet the Greek view is an intelligible one, the basis of which can be easily seen.   Man is a creature of desires and passions, and he is also a creature of

reason. Clearly it is reason that rules, for except in a
few isolated cases a man thinks before he acts, and
his thinking seems to determine his action. Now
when a man thinks, he seems always to be right or
wrong, and of course it is his business to be right. So
an examination of the mechanism of action seems to
show that a man is meant to do the right thing. But
when a man further reflects on his actions, he
recognises that he has often been wrong in the past,
and he also notices that certain other people seem to
know more about the problems involved than he does.
Now, if it is his business in action to do what is right,
and the above considerations seem to show that this
is so, he will act on the opinions of wiser people, since
he knows that they are more likely to be right than
he is ; that is to say, in the words of Plato, " a man
when he is most truly himself will act in accordance
with the best reason, whether it be his own or in some-
body else."   So, again, we return to the ideal of the
Philosopher King, the supremely wise man who is to
find out for us what is right and whose ordinances we
must obey, since in him we recognise Right Reason.

The position may be summed up thus : " There is
an Eternal Truth, an Eternal Justice. These eternal
verities we have to find so as to live our lives in the
light of them. But they are One, and when they are
found, they are found, and it matters not who found
them, for they will shine upon us all and illumine our
lives.   Let us seek out a great philosopher who will
find them for us, and we will live in his shadow."
This was the Greek faith.   Any man who could offer
his disciples the Truth about the Universe in one short
sentence always found many followers in Athens.

We must not assume, however, that Truth and Justice were recognised and worshipped by the Greeks, any more than by other peoples, without a struggle. The very view that the State has an ethical end to serve has at all times had its enemies, and it was only after much toil and many blunderings that the Greeks discovered that there was a fundamental verity underlying the chances and changes of political life, in the light of which the lessons of these changes could be learnt, and the continuity of human progress assured. For even the Greeks, with all their sharpness of intellect and speculative energy, required experience to teach them that it is only in the light of man's ethical judgment that political society can be understood. A brief examination of the political development of Athens is necessary to make this clear.

It was early recognised in Athens that every citizen must have some part in the government of his State ; and the uncompromising and vigorous character of the Athenians soon assured that every citizen could in practice play a real part. So Athens became a democracy. It is to the history of this democracy and its subsequent acts that we must look if we are to determine the Athenian conception of the State ; if we are to discover how far the true meaning of liberty, which seems so admirably exemplified in the growth of their constitution, was really understood by the Athenian people. Clearly they realised that it was necessary to political liberty that every citizen should have a say in the government of the country, but did they know more about it than this ? We have already indicated that the great contribution of the Greeks was that they came to recognise that the business of the State is to make possible the good life, and that all political action and development must be relative to the ethical end of man ; but the time for this conviction had not yet come. We must examine how the light dawned in the history of the Athenian democracy.

We have to deal with a people who governed themselves by means of a General Assembly consisting of all the citizens. What are the principles which should guide the actions and decisions of this Assembly, whose vote alone determined what action should be taken, since there was no other means by which the nation could act ?

On the side of credit we may set the Persian War and the Confederacy of Delos. The democracy at Athens does seem to have recognised a certain duty to drive back the Persians, and, in subsequent years, to protect the islands from Persian aggression. Here the Athenian people seem to have been moved by definite feelings of duty. They might have made extremely advantageous terms with the Persians, but they preferred to stand by the Greek race even at the cost of leaving their city ; and their action has been admired in all ages. Moreover it is established beyond all doubt that in the early years of the Delian Confederacy Athens treated her allies with scrupulous fairness and sometimes even with considerate generosity.

Consider, next, the magnificent building schemes of Athens under Pericles ; these schemes, the nobility of their conception and execution, and the persistence and steadfast judgment which thought it right thus to spend large sums of money over a number of years are unimpeachable evidence of a lofty conception of the purpose of the State. Indeed, the whole of the remarkable career of Pericles bears witness to such a conception. Both this policy and the means which he employed show that he was a man of strong moral judgment and spiritual purpose appealing, on the whole with success, to that side of the Athenian character which was like his own.

"This man," says Thucydides, "deriving authority from his capacity and acknowledged worth, being also a man of transparent integrity, was able to control the multitude in a free spirit : he led them rather than was led by them ; for, not seeking power by dishonest arts, he had no need to say pleasant things, but, on the strength of his own high character, could venture to oppose and even to anger them. When he saw them unreasonably elated and arrogant, his words humbled and awed them ; and when they were depressed by groundless fears, he sought to reanimate their confidence. Thus Athens, though still in name a democracy, was in fact ruled by her greatest citizen." [1]

The Greeks were, however, passing through a difficult time. Their early faith and all their accepted opinions were being weighed in the balance and found wanting. Greek religion was found to be based on a theology which was not merely childish but definitely degenerate in character. Old wives' tales and superstitious explanations were being discredited in the light of the discoveries of science ; and all things, valuable and degrading alike, were being trampled on in the onward march of all-conquering Reason, which could and would explain everything.

This fearless application of Reason to all things sacred and profane has been for all ages the glory of

[1] Thucydides, II., 65.

B 2

the Hellenic world ; and it was to culminate in a
great system of Ethical Philosophy to which even
Christianity owes much, and a great part of which it
has hardly transcended. But the time of this certain
conviction was not yet. The great thinkers were
bound to start by destroying. National beliefs must
yield to doubt, and time was needed before doubt
could yield to knowledge. Meanwhile no guide could
be trusted and there was no criterion to which appeal
could be made. Thus, though the popular sentiment
as to what was right might be a mistaken one, it was
subject to no test, for there was no standard by which
to test it. In default of any accepted morality what
the whole people asserted to be right must be taken
to be right. It was impossible to raise an outcry by
reference to any accepted canons of justice ; everything was in doubt, no view could be proved, and
Reason in the heyday of its newly-found power
would accept nothing but proof. The only thing
which could be recognised was the actual judgment
of the people in any particular case. So at last it
came to be explicitly stated that the people were the
seat of the knowledge of good and evil ; and it was
thought that it must be so and that it was right that
it should be so. There was and there could be no
appeal against the judgment of the whole people ;
no redress from their wrongs except by treason.
There were philosophers to teach that there is and
can be no law superior to that of the State, for above
the law stands the law-giver, and it was the people
of Athens who were her law-givers. So they came to
think it monstrous that they should be unable to do
anything which they wished to do. By playing on

their emotions it was possible to appeal against their decisions, but it was not possible to appeal to principles. They had not even principles to guide their own action—they condemned a whole city to death and then pardoned it on consecutive days—and so the people became the "many-headed capricious beast" of Plato. It is a commonplace that this absence of principle plunged the Athenian people headlong on the road to ruin. This is the story told with such power and judgment by the historian Thucydides. He shows that, in the absence of any law to control their action, the people were bound to end in maintaining and even in believing the philosophy of might. To make this clear it is only necessary to quote from the Melian Dialogue, where Thucydides represents the Athenian embassy as speaking as follows:

"We Athenians will use no fine words; we will not go out of our way to prove at length that we have a right to rule, because we overthrew the Persians; or that we attack you now because we are suffering any injury at your hands. We should not convince you if we did. . . . But you and we should say what we really think, and aim only at what is possible, for we both alike know that into the discussion of human affairs the question of justice only enters where the pressure of necessity is equal, and that the powerful exact what they can, and the weak grant what they must. . . . For of the Gods we believe, and of men we know, that by a law of their nature wherever they can rule they will. This law was not made by us, and we are not the first who have acted upon it; we did but inherit it and shall bequeath it to all time, and we know that you and all mankind, if you were as strong as we are, would do as we do." [1]

[1] Thucydides, V., 89, 105.

In this way the emancipated people of Athens became a tyrant and met its inevitable doom. It remained for Plato to point the moral of its fall and to provide a new inspiration for the future, for in the eyes of the ancients the names of " freedom " and " democracy " were for ever discredited as political ideals.

In the *Republic* Plato at once attacks the heart of the problem, though the question he asks himself is not at first sight a political one. "What is Justice?" he asks, and at once engages with the arch enemy. " Justice is the interest of the stronger." This view, which Plato found so difficult to refute, is put into the mouth of the sophist Thrasymachus. If you examine human nature, he says, you will find that man both does and must act always in his own interest. You have only to look at the actions of those around you to see that this is so ; rulers rule for their own interest—to keep themselves in power and to make themselves rich or loved and respected, according to their private inclination ; and even the shepherd who shows such loving care for the lost lamb is fattening it for his table or for the market. Moreover, what other principles of action can there be ? If you examine the so-called principles of justice and equity in the light of which those men who are reputed good lead their lives, you will see that they are just the convenient regulations of organised society—that the weak have banded together to protect themselves against the strong. When we say that we " ought " not to do so and so, we mean that society forbids us to do it, and that we shall be punished if we do do it ; though of course if we could do it and escape punishment, we should pursue our own advantage all the time, and should be foolish not to do so.

Plato first shows that this argument is self-contradictory, or at least that it will not fit the ordinary use of language ; but though by this preliminary bout Thrasymachus is reduced to silence, Plato does not rest satisfied. He recognises, as he explains at length in a later dialogue, the *Parmenides*, that to show that a view is self-contradictory is an easy task for any sophist, but is in itself valueless to a philosopher except in so far as it suggests to him the basis for a constructive view. He then goes on to remind us that the plain man is confounded by the subtlety of the sophist's view, yet far from being convinced by it, he revolts from it. Plato raises up for us two plain men, Glaucon and Adimantus, who state the view again even more thoroughly and more consistently than did Thrasymachus, but who want to see it refuted. Though they find no flaw in the argument, yet they feel it to be wrong. Plato wants us to see that difficult as the search is—and we shall find it will involve us in an enquiry into the whole nature of truth and reality—yet we must pursue it, for the sceptical view quite clearly will not do ; and since there is a principle of right and wrong we must discover it. It pleased Plato that two men, even creatures of his own fancy, could maintain their faith in the essential goodness of the world in the face of the advance of the all-destroying Reason.

" I have always admired the characters of Glaucon and Adimantus, but when I heard this I was quite extraordinarily pleased and said : ' Children of Thrasymachus though you are, that was a happy reference Glaucon's lover made to you in his elegy, when you distinguished yourselves at the battle at Megara : Sons of Ariston, children divine of a goodly father.' That seems to me very true, my friends, for there is assuredly something divine in you if you are not persuaded that injustice is better than justice when you can speak so eloquently on its behalf." [1]

The preservation of such a faith is for Plato worthy of infinite patience, infinite labour : There is always a fundamental conviction of this sort, attacked by " reason run riot," which underlies all Plato's great philosophical work. There are for him some convictions so deep, so fundamental, that we ought to die rather than give up the attempt to establish them by sound reasoning.

" ' The greater my confidence in you,' says Socrates in the dialogue to Glaucon and Adimantus, ' the less do I feel that I know how to meet the situation. I cannot come to the rescue. I do not think it is in me. Indeed, you convince me of it. For I thought I had proved that justice is better than injustice in my argument with Thrasymachus which you have rejected. And yet I cannot refuse to come to the rescue. I fear it would be impious were I to stand by and refuse aid while justice was being reviled, and did not come to her rescue so long as there was breath in my body, and I had voice to speak. It is best, therefore, that I succour her as well as I can.' " [1]

This is the greatness of Plato : he never rested satisfied with any view however reasonable, if it

[1] Plato, *Republic*, Bk. II., 368.

would not square with the facts of experience,
particularly the facts of spiritual experience. And
Plato was a man of deep spiritual experience. Thus
he found the faith to hold to views which he knew he
could not state ; views which when stated in their
most careful and elaborate form—the result of years
of labour—he could himself " refute " in a few
minutes. Thus it was that one of the clearest thinkers
the world has seen so frequently resorted to myths,
and thus it has come about that if you want to know
Plato's answer to his question, " What is Justice ? "
you must study the *Republic* as a whole. There
is no single sentence, no single paragraph even,
which gives more than a hint of his meaning.

Plato now sets out to succour justice by taking up
the search for a positive answer to his question, for
if he is really to refute the pernicious view of the
sophist he must have a definite view of his own which
will finally convince men that Thrasymachus was
wrong. How will he be able to do this when he has
just confessed himself completely at a loss, and when
he has nothing on which to build, except the feeling
that the sophist's account will not do ? Characteristically he goes right to the root of the matter at
once.   Since the basis of Thrasymachus' view is
that if we examine human nature we find nothing at
the bottom of it as a motive for action but desire and
the calculation of self interest, let us, says Plato, set
before our eyes men living their daily lives—let us
include in our picture everything that seems necessary
to a full life, to the satisfaction of all a man's desires
and inclinations and feelings, and let us then see if
the sophist's account is a true one.   Let us found a

society of men living a full and happy life, and let us look there for justice, in the confident expectation that it will be something far different from the picture Thrasymachus has drawn of it. . . . "If in our argument we were to watch a city in the making should we not see its justice and injustice in the making too ? " So Plato proceeds straightway to his task.

"The origin of a city," he says, "is due to the fact that no one of us is sufficient to himself. Men being in want of many things gather into one settlement many partners and helpers, one taking to himself one man, one another, to satisfy their common needs. And when they exchange with one another, giving or receiving as the case may be, each man thinks that such exchange is for his own good. Thus civil society is the outcome of our necessity." [1]

So Plato enumerates the chief necessities of life and throws into his city butchers and bakers and candlestick makers—craftsmen to supply all the material needs of men and to keep his citizens well supplied and comfortable.

In this way Plato's search for his ideal city seems to be coming to a rapid and easy conclusion.

"Let us consider," he says, "what will be the manner of life of men so equipped ? Will they not spend their time in the production of corn and wine and clothing and shoes ? And they will build themselves houses : in summer they will generally work without their coats, but in winter they will be well-clothed and shod. For food they will make meal from their barley and flour from their wheat, kneading the one and baking the other :

---

[1] Plato, *Republic*, Bk. II., 369.

then they will heap their noble scones and loaves on
reeds or fresh leaves and lying on couches of bryony and
myrtle boughs will feast with their children, drink wine
after their repast and sing hymns to the gods. So they
will live with one another in happiness, not begetting
children above their means, and guarding against the
danger of poverty or war. Leading so peaceful and
healthy a life they will naturally attain to a good old age,
and at death leave their children to live as they have
done." [1]

But Plato knows that this will not do, and at once
he puts his objection through the mouth of Glaucon—

" Why, if you had been founding a city of pigs,
Socrates, this is just how you would have fattened
them ! " [1]

Man was not meant merely to fill his belly and sleep
like the beasts that perish, and then to die leaving
such another life to his children after him. What it
is that is missing Plato does not profess to know at
all accurately ; and so he must throw into his city
all the things which are present in our daily life,
since otherwise his city would not be a real city, and
his view of justice would be drawn from improper
data. He must, therefore, include every detail of
every side of life, in case he should happen to be
omitting something relevant to his search for justice.
It is worth while to follow Plato closely for a little :—

" Very well," he says, " I understand we are considering apparently the making not of a city merely but
of a luxurious city. And perhaps there is no harm in
doing so. From that kind too we shall soon learn, if we

[1] Plato, *Republic*, Bk. II., 372.

examine it, how justice and injustice arise in cities. I
for my part think that the city I have described is the
true one—what we may call the city in health. But if
you wish let us also inspect a city which is suffering from
inflammation. There is no reason why we should not." [1]

The value of this precaution on Plato's part is to be
seen later when it will appear that the good and happy
man is not primarily concerned at all with the
material needs either of himself or of anybody else.
So again and again Plato is saved from holding an
incomplete view by putting before himself a fair and
full picture of the facts, drawn from life, and by
taking his conclusions from that.

Plato thus finds it necessary to make his city much
larger, and it becomes clear that if a large and
elaborate society of this kind is to work smoothly and
well, the division of labour must be worked out so
that everything that is necessary should be done, and
done thoroughly and at the right time. To this end
there must be, broadly speaking, three classes in the
State ; artisans to provide for the material needs of
the citizens, warriors to protect the State from
enemies without and to keep order within, and, lastly,
" Guardians " to rule and govern the State. All these
must practise their own trade and no other, and they
must be carefully and thoroughly trained for this
purpose ; for only so can the various tasks be well
performed, and the city enjoy peace and happiness.

If we now examine this city to see what it is that
makes it good we shall at once discover where justice
lies. It is evidently in the nature of organised society

[1] Plato, *Republic*, Bk. II., 372.

that what is required for its successful working is that every one should know his business and should do it.

" For at the beginning when we were founding our city the principle which we then stated should rule throughout was, I think, Justice, or at least a form of it. We stated surely, and, if you remember, have often repeated our statement, that each individual should pursue that work in this city for which his nature was most fitted, each man doing one work." [1]

If we have to decide what virtue it is which by its presence does most to make a city good, it would seem to be—

" this principle abiding in child and woman, in slave and freeman and artisan, in ruler and ruled, that each minded his own business—one man one work—and was not meddlesome." [1]

This is the principle which makes a city a good and happy state, and the citizens within it good and happy men.

We are now beginning to see some tangible result of Plato's enquiry. We see that he is, in fact, giving the lie direct to Thrasymachus' position. It is wrong to say that at the bottom of human nature there is no governing principle other than desire and self-interest. If we examine the nature of man living a full life in an organised society,—and it is only so that a man can live a full life—we find at the bottom of human nature not some inclination to pursue, not something pleasant to realise, but a task to perform a duty to do. By the performing of this task, and by

[1] Plato, *Republic*, Bk. IV., 433.

that alone can a man be good and find happiness; for
his true happiness must depend on that of the society
in which he lives; and it is only on this condition
that a society can be successful or happy, that every
member fill his allotted place and do his appointed
task.   This is the only road to goodness and to
happiness; only in the good State can a man be good,
only in the happy State can a man be happy.   All
other roads are a deception and a cheat.   By following them a man may gain the pleasure of the moment,
the illicit gain which gives him power to satisfy
immediate desires; but sooner or later comes dis-
illusionment and misery, for even if a man should be
able to escape punishment from gods as well as from
men, yet he cannot escape the results of his own
action.   The only way by which a man can attain
peace at the last is by doing the task allotted him.

Man, then, is not merely a creature of desire.   He
is a being with an allotted task which must guide his
actions throughout his life.   For every man there is a
task to perform, for every occasion there is a right
thing to do, and every agent, however uncontrolled
his power, however sovereign his will, must find this
principle which is writ in the nature of things and
follow it, or it must needs destroy him.   The sovereign
people of Athens itself had a task to perform and a
place in the world to fill, and even Athens could not
escape the results of her evil actions; and so she fell,
destroyed by the principle of justice which she had
repudiated.

It is clear that in order to complete the enquiry
Plato must now go on to discover what are these
great principles of justice which belong to the very

nature of things, and which men and states alike must follow if they are to be good and happy. Plato opens this enquiry by asking what should be the task of the Guardians and what form their education ought to take ; but he is clearly trying to find an answer to the question, " What end ought the State to serve, and what principles ought to guide its action ? " It is Plato's attempt to deal with this problem that gives its chief value to the *Republic*.

Plato sees this question as such a universal and all-embracing one—he sees himself involved in a modification and restatement of all his metaphysical views—that we shall be unable to follow him here in detail.

But his general position is clear. The principle that governs the allotting to every man his task, the principle that makes one object better than another, one action better than another ; the principle that makes one action right for a man to do and another action wrong, one policy right for a nation to pursue and another policy wrong ; the principle, in a word, of justice or "the Good" is part of the fundamental constitution of the universe—it is the principle that makes the world a unity. Only by keeping our eyes fixed upon the Good can we understand the universe, and only by understanding the universe can we comprehend the Good ; and it is the Good shining on our judgment and guiding it through all its difficulties which shows us what it is right for us to do, and also gives us the desire and the strength to do it.

Thus the Guardians must be philosophers. There can be no rules to guide the action of states or of individuals. If a young Guardian ask for rules which shall guide his policy, show him the starry heavens above, teach him the infinite variety of number and of space, let him hear the glory of noble music, let him think of the problems of Truth and of Beauty, and finally let him contemplate the Form of the Good itself. Then he will no longer ask of you a rule, for he will have the knowledge which transcends all rules—the only kind of knowledge there is.

Thus there is a duty for every state and for every man to find out and to do, and only the philosopher can comprehend it. It is clear, then, that the philosopher must rule, for only he can form a true judgment of what the State must do, and it is only by doing what it is right for it to do that it can survive and be just and happy; only if it is so ruled can it fill its place in the order of nature. It will define to every man his place within it; his business will become clear to him and he will find justice and happiness in doing it. Thus in the State, and in the State alone, the spheres and duties of different men are fitted into an harmonious and complete whole. So long as every man performs his task the harmony remains, and peace and happiness reign for the State as a whole and for man, woman and child within it. Only within such an organised and intelligible whole can a man, however wise he be, see his duty clear before him; only then can he know whether his labour is of value, or is wasted.

Thus a decision in practical life can never be in the end a question of desire or of inclination; it is a question of fact—of what will succeed and what will not succeed,—and a question of value—of what is good and what is not good. And for Plato these form, in the end, the same question, and it is only within a State working reasonably and harmoniously that the question can be answered and the calculation made.

Thus the answer to Plato's question, " What is Justice ? " has proved so difficult that Plato has been forced by his line of thought into setting up the philosopher king. Only the philosopher who is specially gifted by nature and who can give his whole time to the contemplation of God and His world can understand justice, and, since without it no state can stand, the philosopher must reign. Under such government the whole problem seems to be solved. For the rulers will see to it that every one within the State is doing the task for which nature has pre-eminently fitted him, and since he is a member of the whole, an essential part of the harmony, he will recognise that the task set him, and nothing else, is his duty and he will do it cheerfully and well. So he, too, by doing his task and by being " just," will be happy.

Naturally, then, for Plato everything must be sacrificed to the harmonious working of the State—a State working as he pictured it with every member doing his work cheerfully and well because he felt it to be peculiarly and properly his own work, and reaping the rewards here and hereafter of those who do their duty. Such a State seemed to Plato so great and so good that nothing that it might be necessary to sacrifice to it could be weighed against it in the balance ; for only in a State and in a just State is justice possible for any man.

The whole problem of morality may then be put in the form—" What must a State be if it is to be able to act justly by its neighbours and so stand as a State, and to work harmoniously within its own borders so that all its members can find their place and their duty within it, and so be just and happy ? "

The first necessity is that every one should have his work ; women, too, then, must have their place to fill. We must make the wives of our guardians take their share in war and in the other duties of guarding the city, and let them do nothing else. Only of these tasks we must assign the lighter to the women, because of the weakness of their sex. For Plato thought that though in some pursuits women tend to excel, and in others men, yet

" there is no one of those pursuits by which the city is ordered which belongs to women as women or to men as men, but natural aptitudes are equally distributed in both kinds of creatures. Women naturally participate in all occupations and so do men, but in all women are weaker than men." [1]

The next conclusion to which Plato's doctrine of the all-importance of the State leads him does not meet with so much sympathy in the modern world as do his views about the education and occupation of women. Nevertheless, it will be seen to be equally necessitated by his general position. There can be no greater evil to a city, argues Plato, than that which rends it asunder, no greater good than that which binds it together and makes it one. Now communion in pleasure and pain binds together a city when, as far as may be, all the citizens rejoice and grieve over common gains and common losses, while,

---

[1] Plato, *Republic*, Bk. V., 455.

on the other hand, it is rent asunder by individuality in these feelings, when one part of the citizens is smitten with grief and the other transported with joy over the same experiences of the city or of its inhabitants.

It would seem, then, that we must banish the words " mine " and " not-mine " from our city, except in so far as they can be pronounced by all the citizens in concert. There must be no private property. No man must have even a wife of his own or any individual family life, for so there would be family set against family, and divisions within the State where all should be of one heart and mind.

All things, then, must be held in common. Such a community we see to be characteristic of that perfect unity—the unity of the individual:

" For consider, when any one of us hurts his finger, the whole fellowship of body and soul which is bound up into a single organism, namely that of the ruling power within it, feels the hurt and is all in pain at once—whole and part together. And so we say that the man has a pain in his finger." [1]

This is the kind of unity at which we must aim in our State.

Of course we may criticise Plato, as Aristotle criticised him, on the ground that he sacrifices the good of the individual to that of the State ; but if we give full weight to his reasoning, we are forced to admit, as Aristotle was forced to admit, that only through the State can there be any good or any good life for the individual. Moreover we must remember

[1] Plato, *Republic*, Bk. V., 462.

that Plato did not think he was sacrificing the good or the happiness of the individual ; in his State every man could and naturally did perform the work and fill the place to which he was fitted by nature, and it was only in so doing, argued Plato, that he could be be good and happy. It did not seem to him to be necessary to the fulfilment of man's nature that he should possess anything which was exclusively his own.

Finally, there is one other doctrine to which Plato was led by his general view which we must consider in some detail. It is clear that there could be no room in Plato's State for Democracy. For Plato every action on the part of the State involved deep and universal problems, the solution of which required an infinitely wise judgment, a mind eternally in contact with Truth and Beauty and Goodness. What could a democracy do in the face of problems such as these ? What is the value of the judgment of " the man in the street " ? How is he to know what is justice and fair dealing ? He cannot have knowledge for he has neither the gift of philosophy by nature, nor the time to practise it ; and, as we have seen, there can be no rules to supply his want of knowledge, since knowledge cannot be put into rules. If, then, the plain man can have no knowledge but only opinion, will not every one have a different opinion ? A state thus divided against itself cannot stand. In a democracy either the city will be divided against itself, or judgment will be unanimous simply because it is swayed by some universal desire or emotion of the moment—and in either case the result must be ruin.

Plato had seen all this in the democracy of Athens

—he had seen it paralysed by differences of opinion at moments when prompt and vigorous action was necessary, and at other times led on to headlong ruin by demagogues playing on its blind emotions. There seemed no place for knowledge in a democracy, and yet without knowledge neither an individual nor a state can stand. What good, then, can there be in a democracy ?

Perhaps Plato overpaints the picture. He thinks of democracy as leading inevitably to the absence of all law and order, though at first sight, he says, it appears good.

" Like a garment of many colours of every shade and variety this constitution will be variegated with every character and be most fair to look upon : and, possibly, just as women and children admire many-coloured things, so many people will judge this city the fairest of all." [1]

Yet, in reality, if we look underneath we see that there is no administration and therefore no harmony in a democracy.

" In this city there is no necessity to rule even if you are capable of ruling, or to be ruled if you do not want, or to be at war because the rest of the city is, or where the rest of the city is at peace to observe peace if you do not wish to . . . It will be, apparently a pleasant constitution, with no rulers and plenty of variety, distributing its peculiar kind of equality to equals and unequals impartially." [1]

It must be admitted that Plato's view has proved its truth again and again—it has throughout history

[1] Plato, *Republic*, Bk. VIII., 557.

been the greatest problem of political development to combine a democratic form of government with an efficient and harmonious administration. If in the modern world we are prepared to sacrifice almost anything in order to secure a democratic form of government, the conclusion would seem to be that we have discovered some hidden virtue in the nature of democracy itself which Plato failed to descry. But we must not be disappointed with Plato because he did not know everything.

Aristotle was a thinker of a different kind. He based his enquiry upon an analysis of wide and detailed information concerning both the practical working of various constitutions and the theories of earlier political thinkers. He loved to commence with a paradox suggested by the consideration of two opposing views, and then to work out a considered statement which should include the truth contained in both. It was perhaps his chief virtue as a thinker that his strong common-sense never allowed him to wander much beyond a cautious analysis of quite concrete difficulties. Aristotle had a natural aversion to mysticism ; and this was perhaps the main cause of the many divergences of opinion which sometimes led him to criticise Plato rather impatiently. For instance, Aristotle rejected the Platonic doctrine of the Form of the Good, partly because he could not understand the theory of the transcendent unity of Reality, and partly because he did definitely think that this view was a positive error arising from a failure to distinguish between things which are different in kind.

For Aristotle every scientific enquiry is different

in kind from every other—arithmetic is arithmetic, and politics are politics, and neither can throw any light upon the other. We must not attempt to draw analogies from one science to another—though of course Aristotle himself was perpetually doing so—for such a method can only lead us into error. Naturally, then, any enquiry is for Aristotle far more narrow and more isolable than it could be for Plato, who thought that a man could not have any real knowledge about arithmetic, for instance, or even about cookery, if he had not thought about the universe as a whole and contemplated the Idea of the Good. Aristotle was very impatient with the method of Plato and thought his work too vague and mystical to have any practical value ; but Plato would no doubt have looked upon Aristotle as a promising pupil still employing himself in studying the subsidiary sciences as a preliminary training before applying himself to the proper work of philosophy itself.

We shall naturally then expect to find that the political enquiry of Aristotle will take a very different form from that of Plato, and will lead to different conclusions. We can perhaps illustrate this briefly by outlining Aristotle's account of Political Justice. His method was to collect and investigate all the available facts relevant to his enquiry and to try to confine himself to drawing only such conclusions as his observations seemed to justify.

" Let us begin," he says, " by considering the common definitions of oligarchy and democracy, and what is justice oligarchical and democratical ? "[1]

[1] Aristotle, *Politics*, III., 9.

For he thinks that oligarchy and democracy must imply different relations between citizen and citizen, and hence different views of Political Justice. " For all men cling to Justice of some kind, but their conceptions are imperfect and do not express the whole idea."

" Justice," he goes on, " is an equality." For him the problem of just dealing can always be put in the form : " How much of the good things of life ought each man to have ? " So in this case he treats the problems of political life as if there were a whole sum of something to be distributed, and as if the question concerned the share to be assigned to each member. In fact, of course, the principle of distribution in any given case will depend on the conditions of association of the claimants and on the nature of the thing to be distributed, but Aristotle is not clear what either of these items is in the case of the State. He can, however, eliminate a good many wrong views and this he proceeds to do.

A state does not exist, he says, simply as an alliance for security against injustice—it is not a mere defensive alliance of the weak against the strong, for in that case all who have commercial treaties with one another would be members of one state ; moreover in the case of an alliance one state does not take care that the citizens of the other are such as they ought to be, but is merely concerned to preserve the actual terms of the treaty, whereas those who care for good government are concerned with the virtue and vice of the citizens.

Thus Aristotle is trying to discover what are the common characteristics of the states under his observation and what these common characteristics imply. He is always primarily concerned to construct a view which is consistent with the relevant facts and he seems always to have made up his mind before he starts what facts are relevant. Within the limits he has set himself Aristotle is wonderfully accurate and exhaustive in his observation and in general he seems to discover all that can be discovered from such observation alone, but the method is a pedestrian one and has obvious dangers, as well as disadvantages that become clear enough if we go to Aristotle for a philosophy of life or even for inspiration.

Nevertheless it will become clear as we proceed that the method has its value and is essential to any enquiry. It may be further inferred from this consideration, he continues, that virtue must be the serious care of a state which truly deserves the name, for without this ethical end the community becomes a mere alliance. It is clear that a state is not a mere collection of men, inhabiting a common territory and united together to prevent crime and to make possible organised exchange. These are no doubt conditions without which a state cannot exist, but all together they do not constitute the State; for its end is the good life to which these can be no more than the means. In a word the state is the union of families and villages having for an end a perfect and self-sufficing life, by which we mean a happy and an honourable one; though it comes into being for the sake of the maintenance of life itself, it is for the sake of the good life that it endures.

Aristotle then goes on to urge that they who

contribute most to such a society have a greater
share in it than those who, though they have the
same or greater freedom or nobility of birth, are
inferior to them in political virtue. In seeking to
discover what kind of man contributes most to the
State Aristotle again does not try to answer the
question himself, but considers in turn the merits
of the various claimants. Seeing that these may
depend on wealth, courage, virtue or the pre-
ponderance of number, he concludes that all have a
claim but none an absolute claim. All these considerations seem to show that none of the principles
on which men claim to rule and to hold all other men
in subjection to them are strictly right.

" To those who claim to be the masters of the State
on the ground of their virtue or of their wealth, the
many might fairly answer that they themselves are often
better and richer than the few. I do not say individually,
but collectively." [1]

It is to be noticed that Aristotle's whole enquiry
is oriented by his assumption that the good, to which
service gives a claim, is ruling. Thus to " contribute " to the State is for him to do something which
will entitle a man to rule ; and this view finds its
logical conclusion in the doctrine that if there be found
a man who himself alone excels in virtue all other
members of the State, he has the right to rule and
to command the obedience of the others—a doctrine
which has been supposed by some to be a concession
to Alexander the Great, but which is in fact a natural
conclusion from Aristotle's general view.

[1] Aristotle, *Politics*, III., 13.

This identification of ruling with the good depends, at best, upon a hasty assumption. Aristotle never seems to have enquired what kind of rule is possible if the State is to serve an ethical end and to promote the good life for each individual within it. The truth is that, as Plato realised, the doctrine that the State serves an ethical end must necessarily modify the whole conception of rule or government ; Plato thought that the only possible rule lay in so organising the State that every one should naturally do what was for the good of the whole State, because it happened to be his business, and in the perfect organisation of the perfect State the task lay ready to his hand. It may be that this is an ideal and that such a State may never be on earth, but for all that Plato seems to be aiming at the solution of a general problem which Aristotle never saw.

But though Aristotle's enquiry, taken as a whole, is thrown into confusion by his failure to raise the general issues which are fundamental to such an investigation, we must not for that reason abandon him prematurely. He is certainly a little hasty in his assumption that the problem of Political Justice is one of distribution, and further that the chief prize in that distribution is " Rule "—he should at any rate have considered the Platonic view that the good which the State has to give is something to do and not something to have, and he should certainly have enquired what he meant by " ruling " before asking who ought to rule. Yet for all this his enquiry is by no means barren, and his general view is clearly sound, that what is right is to be considered by reference, not to any past implied contract or to any standing conferred by birth or wealth, but by reference to the advantage of the State and the common good of the citizens.

Moreover it is hardly necessary to say that as the result of his exhaustive observation Aristotle let fall so much wisdom on particular points that his work has been the wonder of succeeding ages. At times he speaks as if he knows all that there is to be known, and says things which so nearly touch the heart of the problem that they defy criticism or improvement. To illustrate this we may refer to the marvellous passage on the authority of law which may be summarised thus :

" Absolute monarchy or the arbitrary rule of a Sovereign over all the citizens in a city which consists of equals is thought by some to be contrary to nature. It is thought to be just that among equals everyone be ruled as well as rule, and that all should have their turn. We thus arrive at law ; for an order of succession implies law. And the rule of law is preferable to that of any individual. There may indeed be cases which the law seems unable to determine, but in such cases, can a man ? He who bids the law rule may be deemed to bid God and Reason above rule, but he who bids man rule adds an element of the beast, for desire is a wild beast, and passion perverts the mind of rulers even when they are the best of men. The law is reason unaffected by desire." [1]

So far there seems no more to be said. Yet Aristotle merely treats this as one view among many, and allows it to pass with the reflection that owing to the innate wickedness of magistrates it is no better in practice than any other ; and fails to draw the con-

[1] Aristotle, *Politics*, III., 16.

clusion that such a view of law comes nearer in
principle than any other view to ensuring that the
State should serve a moral purpose.

Finally there is one principle in respect of which
Aristotle does mark a quite definite and important
advance on Plato. He emphasised the fact that it is
not the sole business of political philosophy to construct an Ideal State over which men may shake their
heads in yearning in secluded speculation; and further that such an Ideal State improperly understood may cause misguided people to act wrongly in
particular cases. If a man wants to know what it is
just for him to do he must consider not the regulations laid down in Plato's *Republic*, for example,
but the laws of his own State; for justice must depend
on the nature of the State to which he belongs.
Justice oligarchical is different from justice democratical and what is just may even vary in different
oligarchies and in different democracies. Aristotle
saw that if every man were always guided by the principle of doing what he thought it would be his duty
to do if he were a member of an Ideal State, instead
of doing what the law and principle of justice in
his own state required of him, then civil society
and therefore the moral life would be impossible.
Aristotle saw that it is not only common sense, but
it is in the highest and strictest sense a man's duty to
do all he can for the state of which he is a member,
and not incontinently to perform actions which will
impede the life and development of that state,
simply because it is not all that it might be.

Thus Aristotle realised that the membership of any
state, however good or however bad, imposes on a

man obligations, and therefore that we cannot tell what a man's duty is without first considering the nature of the state to which he belongs. To take an example, if Socrates lived the life he did without troubling to consider whether better institutions were likely to be raised in place of those institutions, political and religious, which by his teaching he brought into disrepute, then he was a bad man ; such action would only be justified if he thought either that better institutions would immediately take their place, or that the existing order was so bad that even a state of complete anarchy would be better for mankind.   It would seem that neither Socrates nor Plato raised for themselves this issue, and here Aristotle marks an important advance.

Political philosophy should consider, says Aristotle, not only what form of government is ideally best, but also what is possible. There are some who would have none but the most perfect, but for this many advantages are required, and meanwhile men must have some form of civil government. It is important for the statesman and the citizen to remember this in all their actions.   " Any change of government which is to be introduced must be one which men will be both able and willing to accept, since there is quite as much trouble in the reformation of an old constitution as in the establishment of a new one." So Aristotle emphasises that in deciding what it is just to do we have to bear in mind the duty of keeping some form of constitution in action all the time. For when we depart from the rule of law we hand over the destinies of the State to the " Beast."

So while Plato showed that there is a problem for

political organisation to solve—that is to say, the establishing of a form of organisation which moral beings can obey—Aristotle saw that mankind has never, so to say, a free hand with the problem, but that while, in his political practice, he keeps one eye on the end to be attained, he must keep the other eye on the maintenance of the ground already won.   It is only by the consideration of both these principles that the problem of political justice can be solved.

CHAPTER II

IN turning from the politics of Greece to those of Rome we are attacking a different problem and one which at first sight is more difficult. In the writings of the Roman philosophers there is little original political thought. Cicero, for example, was concerned rather to understand the Greek thinkers than with speculation of his own ; while Seneca was too deeply imbued with Stoic doctrines to be able to learn the lessons which the political practice of his time might have taught him.

Yet we cannot leave Rome out of the reckoning, for she succeeded in governing the world in almost unbroken peace for four centuries, and in laying the foundations of all subsequent development of law, civil and international alike. So, in the absence of any theory, we must examine her practice if we are to discover Rome's contribution to political progress, to learn the lesson of her success and to point the moral of her fall.

In the early days of their history the Romans were too busy struggling for life itself to be able to occupy themselves with the problems of the " good life." The early history of Rome is a tale of continuous war. When we remember that the Romans were farmers and that it was with difficulty that they could tend their crops and fight a war at the same time, we shall understand that the ever-present fear of discomfort and even of starvation for their families prevented them from speculating in the market-place about their rights and privileges. Thus we find developing in the Roman character a natural adherence to tradition which only the most unavoidable necessity could stir to such action as might lead to political advance ; and since on the whole the governing class of these early days knew the art of yielding, the Roman people grew definitely content with the main principles of their constitution, until it gradually came about that it should never occur to them that things might be otherwise. So the steady persistence in maintaining the old order, which was always characteristic of the Romans, was in part the natural outcome of their early history. They were too busy with external problems of defence and later of expansion to contemplate any internal change except when the need was imperative ; and thus they grew to full political maturity with the principles of their primitive state firmly embedded in their character. These principles they never abandoned. There always remained among them, for instance, a strong family feeling, a strong class feeling, and, most characteristic of all, a strong patron and client feeling, which survived to the latest days of the Empire. Their natural and inbred conservatism gave an extraordinary unity to the Roman State ; it was characteristic of the Romans that during nearly three centuries of political struggling no blood was shed in civil strife.

During this period the Romans showed in general a remarkable justness of dealing in their wars. They were strict in their adherence to treaties and recognised that their word when once given was binding. It may be well to illustrate the severity of their moral principles by two familiar stories, which, whether or not they are true, show clearly enough what qualities the Romans were used to admire. In 278 B.C. Pyrrhus, king of Epirus, had already won two crushing victories over the Roman armies. There could be no reasonable doubt that unless he was killed or left Italy he would carry the war up to the walls of Rome and perhaps sack the city itself. One of the royal servants came to the consul Fabricius, who was in command of the Roman forces, and offered to poison his master if he were promised a reward. Fabricius at once sent him back to Pyrrhus as a prisoner, disdaining to take a mean advantage of a noble foe.

Again, less than half a century later, when the first Punic war had lasted for ten years, and Rome was practically exhausted, a large part of her field army was annihilated before Carthage, and Regulus, the Roman commander, fell into the hands of the enemy. He was despatched to Rome by the Carthaginians to convey their terms of peace, under the condition that he should return to Carthage if his efforts were unsuccessful. When he appeared before the Senate, instead of urging the acceptance of the Carthaginian offer, he insisted that Rome should reject it and continue the war, since Carthage, though apparently triumphant, was in fact no less exhausted than her opponent. He carried his point. Peace was refused, and Regulus, true to his word, returned voluntarily to meet his death by torture at the hands of his enemies.

This sense of a supreme principle governing the

conduct of nations and individuals alike was always present in the minds of the Romans. They recognised that there was a law which must control the actions of a nation, however powerful and triumphant, and they were prepared to admit that even subject peoples had rights. So on the whole they showed clemency; they interfered as little as possible with the forms of government of the nations which they conquered and gradually extended to them privileges within the Roman commonwealth itself, and finally admitted them to citizenship.

No doubt the Romans did not make war for merely moral reasons. Of course, being practical persons, they dodged their consciences at times with quibbling arguments. But they genuinely felt, and to a great extent acted on, their principles. There is no doubt that it was largely owing to their moral principles that they won and secured the hegemony of Italy. First, they recognised that a nation should never make war "iniuria"—that is, it should never make a purely aggressive war to gratify selfish interests or desires, but only when itself or its allies had been wronged. Secondly, they were always prepared to support friends and allies in their just quarrels. Thirdly, they thought that the victor should use his right as conqueror with clemency, and should only proceed to extremities against those who had proved themselves to be inveterate and dangerous enemies.

These principles were rather inherent in the working of the Roman state than a definite doctrine propounded by philosophers or orators. As has been pointed out before, it seems very rarely to have occurred to the Romans to speculate on the general

principles underlying conduct. Their absence of
political consciousness is finally witnessed by their
constitutional development. During all this period
of external expansion Rome was ruled by an
aristocratic government, the working of which
entirely depended on the probity and patriotism of
the governing class. The lower classes rather assumed
that their needs would be attended to than made
efforts to secure this by constitutional measures ; and
during the two hundred years of its greatness the
Roman Senate ruled well, and this not because of any
enlightened political theory, but because of the principles bred in the bone of the Roman aristocrat.
While the nobles were acknowledged to have a special
claim to high office and the governance of the State,
the other classes had their claims no less. It was
very strongly felt that the free poor ought not to be
oppressed, and that life should be made tolerable for
them ; and it was a tradition that the State should
use the public land as a fund out of which to provide
from time to time for the superfluous poor. These
claims were generally recognised in practice. It was
always a principle governing Roman administration
that the well-born and the rich should govern under
the obligation of making things comfortable for the
poor.

This simple, unsophisticated form of government
by the Senate, which chiefly depended on the public
spirit of the senators, broke down under the strain of
Imperial administration. When the Romans came
to rule peoples outside Italy, they did mean to apply
the same principles and maintain the same homely
form of government, based on the virtues of the

governors they sent out. But the wealth and luxury
of the conquered peoples were too much for the
simple Roman. There was no central government
under the Republic capable of controlling the provincial governors and tax-farmers, and these, "having
enormous opportunities for plunder and appetites
and energies strengthened by ancestral puritanism,"
were unable to control themselves. A different
system was needed for the administration of an
empire.

It was characteristic of the Romans that as a
nation they never really learned this lesson. Through
a century of terrible bloodshed they tried to re-estab-
lish their old form of government unchanged. Even
the reformers who arose in a long succession one
after another only toyed with the problem. It did
not occur to them that their world empire required a
completely new organisation, a new system of government. They looked back to the golden age of their
forefathers and, recognising its outstanding virtues,
saw in the principles of the old republicanism their
only Utopia. They thought, as many men have
thought in all ages, that there was no problem in the
life either of the individual or of the State which
could not be solved by the common sense of the
plain man ; and they thought that the only possibility of good government lay in the goodness of
individual rulers. It was on these principles that
Cicero stood in his heroic attempt to establish again
a firm order of things. He called for all good men and
true to rally to his standard ; and he sought to set
up a stable government by the balancing of the
aristocracy and the upper middle class, both of whom

must be aiming (so he thought) solely at the good of the State. For him there was no aim but the good of the State ; this was the end of all ambition ; and it was the proudest moment of his life when he was saluted as " father of his country." But Cicero was a " new man," and came of fresh blood ; and such men were greatly outnumbered in Roman politics by the representatives of a largely degenerate aristocracy. Moreover, it was becoming clear at last that something more than a mere rude virtue was necessary for the ruling of an empire. Yet, apart from the selfish desires of some adventurers, there were no fresh ideas in Roman politics, and therefore no driving force behind movements of reform.

The time came, however, when a new form of government was forced on the people of Rome. By the labours of Julius and Augustus Cæsar the needed central government was established. It was still necessary, indeed, that the omnipotence of the central power should be shrouded under the forms of the old republicanism ; there were still consuls and tribunes elected annually, and the Emperor was in principle merely the first citizen in the state ; but in fact there was no appeal against the imperial power.

Henceforward we find one man swaying the world, often by his own caprice, and that caprice frequently vicious. The power of the Emperor was arbitrary even when it was most wisely employed. Yet the Roman Empire rendered greater services to the cause of liberty than the Republic had done. At home the poor enjoyed the comfort and security that they had demanded in vain of the Republic ; abroad we find the blessings of the Pax Romana. Moreover, to the

Imperial period belongs the greater part of Roman literature, and almost the entire civil law. For nearly four centuries there was very little rebellion within the Empire, and few serious wars on its borders; the municipalities were happy and contented, and the world was at peace. And meanwhile the Emperor might fiddle and Rome burn.

Wherein lies the secret? If we may believe Tacitus and Juvenal, the Imperial court often reached depths of tyranny and vice such as can hardly have been rivalled in the history of the world. Yet the nations worshipped Rome and built temples to the deified Emperors. What cared they for the private life of the Emperor? What was it to them that life was impossible for the old Roman nobility, and that all the ablest men in the capital were being cut off through the animosities and caprices of the ruler and of his favourites?

> " For forms of government let fools contest,
>   Whate'er is best administered is best."

The administration of the Roman Empire was, and is, a pattern and an inspiration to the world.

In every part of the Empire, state and individual alike were given something to aim at, something to do. The state, when it first entered the Empire, was allowed to keep its own constitution, though it paid taxes; but it might hope, by good behaviour, to become a municipium, with a form of government on the Roman model and with rights and privileges granted by charter. The individual might gain honour by holding office in his own town or country, and he might in some favoured states become a full Roman

citizen by holding the highest office in his munici-
pality. There were also religious offices which carried
social prestige, and even some recognition in Rome.

The important point about this organisation, however, was not its completeness, but the fact that it
was acceptable.   There was something about the
Roman constitution and the Roman character which
made states extremely anxious to gain a constitution
on the Roman model and become " municipia," and
which made individuals eager to find favour in the
sight of Rome and to become Roman citizens. It is
clear from inscriptions that generation after generation of hardy and able men in all parts of the world
lived content to give all their energies to the struggle
for these Roman honours, and died content to have
gained them. And these people were happy in their
generation ; they were prosperous and contented and
had a large measure of freedom ; they were free to
strive for what they wanted, and the rewards of their
labours were granted and withheld with equal justice
to all. It is the Roman glory that the ends which the
world desired could be attained without sacrificing
the organised peace and happiness of the world.

At first, no doubt, there was a darker side. The
Roman system, while it provided admirable securities
for the rights of citizens, allowed a savage disregard
for the rights of man. The free Roman was allowed
to inflict atrocious wrongs on his children, and on
his dependents and slaves. Gradually, however, the
broader conceptions of justice and equity which were
so familiar to the generous minds of Greece gained a
sway over the thoughts of men, and all was mellowed
by Christianity. A general spirit of friendliness pre-

vailed to crown the economic success and material comfort achieved by Roman organisation. Thus in the provinces under Roman rule at its best we find more than a hint of the Platonic ideal ; there was a place for every state and for every man, and in general both alike fitted happily and contentedly into that place. No one need be idle ; no one need be destitute. Throughout the world there prevailed a contented, old-fashioned, unprogressive village life, and, of course, the world was happy.

Evidently, then, the political theorist has much to learn from Rome. It must be his task to discover how it was that Rome succeeded in making the various nations under her sway content to fit into her form of government ; for, as far as the assurance of peace and contentment is concerned, the Roman rule seems to have been as successful as any the world has seen.

It is a commonplace to suggest that the success of Rome was chiefly due to her magnificent system of law. This system provided, as it were, a solid core in the Roman commonwealth, which was permanent, reliable and intelligible. Even the brilliant and enterprising Athenians learned by experience that, in the long run, what is of most value in a government is solid virtue and reliability ; so it came about that, in spite of some fickleness, they maintained Pericles in power and supported his policy right up to his death ; and so it was that the dull-witted and unenterprising Nicias could command a support which Alcibiades, with all his brilliant gifts and lavish promises, could never obtain. So it was in the Roman Empire.

In personal and private life the provincial found under Roman rule all the solidity and permanent security which he could desire. He could regard all the petty affairs of private and municipal life as secure and calculable. His life was governed not by the caprice of an emperor or even of a Roman governor, but by the justice of the law courts. When he appealed to or was led before the courts, he was certain of justice according to the law, and the law he knew. The government was giving him, in fact, the first great thing which a man demands of his government—a reasonable security and a calculable regularity in his daily affairs. In a State whose government so far succeeds in its task nearly all things are possible.

It was the law court which really stood for the Roman Government to the ordinary provincial. The Emperor and Rome were far away ; yet these names no doubt inspired a certain awe, and perhaps even a certain affection, which contributed something towards maintaining loyalty. At least the emperors thought that this was so, and they tried to foster the worship of their deified predecessors, and even of themselves while yet on the throne. It would seem, moreover, that this attempt was not unsuccessful ; emperor worship maintained itself for over three centuries against Christianity and Mithraism alike, and when ultimately it was combined with the former as the official religion of the Empire, it modified very considerably the religion which appeared entirely to displace it.

It was chiefly, however, by far more solid forces that loyalty was maintained. Emperors might come and go, but the great system of Roman law remained for ever, and offered benefits which no one would lightly throw away—benefits which, indeed, in a few generations established themselves so firmly in the hearts and minds of men that they came not even to think or dream of any other order of things. This is what Tacitus means when he says that the Roman rule " corrupted " the provincials ; the Romans spread " humanitas," chiefly because the " humanitas " made the world easier to govern. But, when all is said, peaceful government is a great boon to give mankind ; and the boon was in itself rendered none the less great by the fact that the Romans enjoyed governing.

In view of its political importance, it will be worth while to examine the development of the great system of Roman law. It was little more than half a century after the expulsion of the kings from Rome when the common people forced from their aristocratic rulers a definition of their political rights in a written code of laws—the celebrated code of Twelve Tables (450 B.C.). The story goes that a deputation was sent to Athens to examine the institutions of Solon in order to be in a better position to arrange and tabulate the rights of the people. The value of this code consisted, however, less in any symmetrical classification or clearness of expression than in the fact that it was published. This publication modified to a remarkable extent the power of the nobles, who had hitherto been the sole expositors of the law as well as its administrators ; but it had the even more important effect of giving a certain solidarity to the Roman constitution, in that the proletariat could now know how they stood, and the issue in political strife could always be the clear and simple one of whether or not to modify or add to the written code ; thus any advantage won by the proletariat could be recorded, and could, therefore, be regarded as won for good. By this step the Romans advanced a great way towards abstracting personal animosity and party rancour from their political struggles. Without a written law, no doubt the only possible way to deal with a government, a part of whose policy is obnoxious to the people at large, is to extirpate the government, thus destroying the good with the bad ; this method naturally involves the necessity of starting from the beginning again to deal with the problem in hand, only too often without any attempt to learn the lesson of the past failure, with the result that the new attempt is likely to add one more failure. This method in politics was developed to its highest level of excellence by the Greeks, and its tragic results were finally exposed in the pages of Thucydides, where the historian offers his Reflections on Factions at Corcyra.

The Romans, on the other hand, by the publication of the code of the Twelve Tables and by the formulation of later political developments in constitutional statutes, started on a different road at the very outset. On their principles, it was only necessary to bring about a change in or an addition to the written code ; the ordinary routine of the law courts would see to it that the law was kept. In this way factions, massacres and assassinations were not necessary, for any particular party or person was powerless against the constitution, and the constitution was known to every one. No doubt it was still possible for a political party to gain great influence by referring to the " mos maiorum " on particular issues, but this could only apply to minor points where the constitution was not clear, or to new issues or difficulties where such a method, in so far as it exhorted men to learn from experience, could do nothing but good. But it would clearly have been impossible to further a political programme by " projecting into the past " the proposed policy and calling it the " constitution of Cleisthenes " or of any early reformer—a procedure which is supposed to have been achieved with some success in Athens. Constitutional struggles could be brought out into the open in Rome and fought on a clear and open issue as between the existing state of things, which was known, and the reformed state of things, which was aimed at ; and the issue of the struggle could be registered in published writing with the assurance that that battle was won once and for all.

The code of the Twelve Tables was fought for and won in order to secure the position of the proletariat against their oligarchical rulers, but it had also another important effect. Coming at an early stage of Roman civilisation, it enshrined the early tribe law and custom of the primitive people of Rome before the sophisticating influence of contact with other civilisations could cause it to be changed or disbelieved in.

Thus it was saved from the fate to which unwritten law is so frequently doomed when the essence is lost and the mere trappings preserved. This the code made impossible, and, in particular, it saved the specifically Roman contribution to law from being swamped once and for all in the wave of intoxication of Greek free-thinking which swept over the slow minds of Rome. It protected Roman law and custom from the " spontaneous depravation and debasement of national institutions." Of this the Roman jurists were very proud, and they sought to preserve the code in all its strictness just because it was the law of their fathers, even when the times had changed or when a fresh light had been thrown on it by their acquaintance with foreign thought and jurisprudence.

Of course, this civil law was only applied to Roman citizens ; from the earliest times foreigners were excluded from the jurisdiction of the civil law no less than from the constitution. This exclusion soon gave rise to difficulties, owing to the large numbers of foreign merchants and craftsmen who were always in Rome.

In the early days these non-citizen residents had, no doubt, sought protection in the hill city from the robber tribes of the surrounding country, and later, as Rome became mistress first of Italy and then of the world, their number naturally increased. The Roman lawyers had then to face the problem of settling disputes among these non-citizens who were excluded from the civil law. They solved the problem by compiling for these cases a special code, which they called the *Jus Gentium* or Law of Nations.

" All nations," says the Institutional Treatise published (A.D. 529) under the authority of the Emperor Justinian, " who are ruled by laws and customs, are

governed partly by their own particular laws and partly
by those laws which are common to all mankind. The
law which a people enacts is called the civil law of that
people, but that which natural reason appoints for all
mankind is called the Law of Nations, because all nations
use it."

The method which the Roman jurists followed in
formulating this law was a simple one. They compared the national laws and customs of all the
surrounding nations with which they came into contact, and selected all that they found to be common
to all these codes. Thus the *Jus Gentium* did not
contain any of the special characteristics of the law
of any one race, but attempted to formulate the
common basic principles on which rest the laws of
all nations.

It must not be supposed that the Romans treated
the *Jus Gentium* with any special respect. To-day,
no doubt, it would be taken for granted that such a
system would be superior to any national civil code
as emanating from a necessarily broader outlook and
excluding national prejudices and irrelevances ; but
this was not at all the Roman point of view. We have
seen that the Romans reserved for citizens the
privilege of the jurisdiction of the Roman Civil Law,
and the *Jus Gentium* was compiled for such as had
not this privilege. It was drawn from national
laws which seemed absurdly mean and unsophisticated in the jurist's eye as compared with the Roman
Civil Law, and it never occurred to the lawyer that
it might be better or nobler than the various national
codes from which it was extracted.

Although the *Jus Gentium* was proffered by the

Roman lawyer with a gesture of contempt, it was none the less acceptable to the foreigner ; in fact, it was in all probability more acceptable than the Roman law would have been. Furthermore, it at once put Rome in a position which no state had before enjoyed, for every one knew the law by which his disputes would be settled, and by which he would be protected or himself condemned in the event of trespass. The Athenians had no doubt meant to deal justly in their courts by foreign merchants, but they got little credit for their efforts, because the foreigner did not understand the Athenian law, and therefore tended to think himself unjustly treated. Rome avoided this by compiling the Law of Nations, and so prepared the way to make herself mistress of the world ; for long before she was in a position of control she had set the standard for international dealings.

The subsequent history of the Law of Nations throws even more light on the greatness of Rome, and explains even further her success in absorbing the nations into a great world State. The time came when the study of the Law of Nations caused such a broad and ample development of Roman Civil Law that any man from any nation might with justice claim to see in the Roman law the idealised form of his own national law, and so feel that he was in no way derogating his national dignity by his proud boast, " Civis Romanus sum."

This crisis arrived, as Sir Henry Maine points out, " when the Greek theory of a Law of Nature came to be applied to the practical Roman administration of the law common to all nations."

" After Nature," he says, " had become a household
word in the mouths of the Romans, the belief gradually
prevailed among the Roman lawyers that the old Jus
Gentium was in fact the lost code of Nature. . . . The
inference from this belief was immediate, that it was the
Prætor's duty to supersede the civil law as much as
possible by the edict, to revive as far as might be the
institutions by which Nature had governed man in the
primitive state. Of course there were many impedi-
ments to the amelioration of law by this agency. There
may have been prejudices to overcome even in the legal
profession itself, and Roman habits were far too tenacious
to give way at once to a mere philosophical theory. The
indirect methods by which the edict combated certain
technical anomalies show the caution which its authors
were compelled to observe, and down to the very days
of Justinian there was some part of the old law which
had obstinately resisted its influence. But, on the whole,
the progress of the Romans in legal improvement was
astonishingly rapid as soon as stimulus was applied to it
by the theory of natural law. The ideas of simplifica-
tion and generalisation had always been associated with
the conception of Nature ; simplicity, symmetry and
intelligibility came therefore to be regarded as the
characteristics of a good legal system, and the taste for
involved language, multiplied ceremonials and useless
difficulties disappeared altogether. The strong will and
unusual opportunities of Justinian were needed to bring
the Roman law to its existing shape, but the ground plan
of the system had been sketched long before the imperial
reforms were effected." [1]

This development took place, of course, through
the ordinary administration and jurisdiction of the
law-courts. Thus the daily life of the Empire was
constructing and developing a great system, which

[1] Maine, *Ancient Law*, Ch. III.

was independent of any person or party or of any one generation, and which might be regarded by all men as a triumph of human progress, a guarantee of peace and order which must be maintained and defended at all costs. It is not remarkable that subject peoples were anxious to take on the citizenship of this great world-wide institution of civilisation, for the old Greek adage, "The men are the city," was given the lie in the understanding of all men. Standing or falling with the Roman State was this great fabric of human learning and human experience—a good which was palpable enough for any man to recognise, since it touched him so nearly in his daily life, a system of law and international dealing which made it possible for the world to live at peace.

Thus Roman organisation brought nearly all that men could desire; but the perfect administration acted as a strong narcotic. It was based rather on the control of power than on the regulation of liberty. It succeeded because by its very greatness it made its subjects look to the State as the only aim and end of all mankind, and to the struggle to serve the State and for advancement within it as the only laudable activity of man. So many prerogatives were concentrated within the State that there was left no footing on which a man could take his stand to deny its jurisdiction or assign bounds to its activity. There was only one legislator and one authority in religion and morality no less than in politics. The conclusion was inevitable: the State claimed the use of all a man's faculties and the determination of all his duties. The most sacred obligations vanished before the public advantage, until in the end the State controlled the very desires of the citizen by providing him with ends to desire.

By such a sacrifice of freedom, organisation and peace were too dearly bought. By her disregard of private interests, by her suspicion and fear of private enthusiasm and enterprise, by her lack of interest in the moral welfare and improvement of the people except in so far as it obviously contributed to easy organisation, Rome destroyed the vital elements on which the prosperity of nations rests, and her empire was bound to fall before the first serious challenge.

A State cannot stand ; it must either develop and grow or decline and fall. Organisation is necessary to civil life, but a State cannot survive if it is organised on the principle of suppressing everything which might make organisation difficult. Political administration must be on the basis of encouraging individual enterprise, and so creating a new task for the administrator and a new situation for him to face. The genius of the Romans lay in their power of inspiring subject peoples not to emulate the Roman constitution by political advance, but to a slavish imitation of the Roman model. So Rome killed the spirit of political inquiry and political enterprise, and the world had to pay the penalty by seven hundred years of darkness.

CHAPTER III

THE MIDDLE AGES : THE INFLUENCE
OF CHRISTIANITY

WE have seen that the Roman genius, while it succeeded in building up an empire which was a model of peaceful administration, had all the while been sapping the vital energy of the peoples under its rule. The unity of the Roman Empire entirely depended on the success of its method of organisation. This method in the end rested on a basis of the elimination of national and racial differences, and with these differences were eliminated also those special ideals and aspirations on which the vitality of peoples depends. Hence, when the inevitable challenge came, there was no force strong enough to hold together or to reunite the disintegrating fragments. A nation might have survived even the barbarian invasions of the fifth century ; a mere organisation lost everything in this catastrophe. So the greatness of Rome became no more than a name, though her name and her memory proved more powerful in death than her living greatness. Her empire, with its faults and its virtues alike, proved a model to the writers and thinkers of the succeeding centuries, a model which they hardly criticised and certainly failed to transcend, though it became more and more evident that it was fatally powerless to assist in shaping any real development in the destinies of the new peoples of the Middle Ages.

The world had lost for ever that perfect organisation which had ensured the peace and prosperity of four centuries ; and if it was ever again to enjoy such an era, it could not be on the basis which had made possible the Roman Empire. But the success of that empire had been so evident that the peoples who had lived securely under its shadow only looked back with regret and gratitude to the comfort and prosperity they had then enjoyed. They could not know that the fall of the Empire was to mark the beginning of a new age—an age in which the peoples of the world were gradually to awaken to the knowledge that there is something more needed in social and individual life than mere organisation and the comfort and security which organisation can give. When once this was recognised, there could be no return to the old order ; there was bound to be an advance, however groping and however slow.

It is to those centuries immediately succeeding the fall of Rome, which history has relentlessly labelled as the Dark Ages, that we must look for the beginnings of a new spirit. Truly they are not years of startling historical or literary achievement. They do not contribute a definitely formulated political theory. Their revolt against the soulless efficiency of Rome takes shape in no dramatic act or utterance. They can boast no thinker of the type of Rousseau to proclaim from the housetops, " Man is born free." Yet it is an idea not far removed from that of Rousseau that underlies their thought, and in the writings of the Christian Fathers, and in the struggles

of the Empire and Papacy, and later in the development of the Nation State, we are conscious of a
striving after its realisation.   The idea is a very
simple one, and it is familiar throughout the whole
Christian world, for it is the message of Jesus Christ.
It is not surprising that Christianity should have
provided the stimulus which was lacking to the
Roman Empire ; rather it seems at first sight surprising that it should not have saved the world from
the Dark Ages before ever they began. A message
such as that of St. Paul—" There is neither bond nor
free, there is neither male nor female ; for ye are all
one in Christ Jesus "—would be expected to strike
to the heart of oppressed peoples. It would naturally
be their problem to find a basis of organisation compatible with this doctrine of individual freedom and
of the high moral purpose of individual life preached
in the New Testament.

This would no doubt have happened had the
nations under the Roman Empire been sufficiently
oppressed ; but, perhaps unfortunately for the
spiritual development of the world, the peoples did
not feel themselves so oppressed.   What they
remembered about the Roman Empire was not so
much its absence of ideas and ideals as its comfort and
administrative success.   Their freedom to struggle
with the new problems was, therefore, hampered by
their consistent attempt to solve them on the basis of
the Roman model—that is, to produce a new world
empire in its unity and administrative principle
similar to that of Rome, but compatible with and
capable of guaranteeing the new ideal of freedom.

The Christian Church made many converts, and

eventually organised its resources so that its rulers were able to make a stand against the rival temporal authority, though naturally this latter part of its influence could only be developed slowly. Christianity showed that its faith could spread further and more swiftly than the temporal power of Rome had spread. But time was needed for an organisation with this faith for its basis to take its position in the life of the world. If we bear in mind that the spreading of the Christian faith and the growing of the power of the Church meant precisely the same thing to the mediæval Christian, and that, therefore, any repudiation of the temporal power of the Church would involve a setting back of the spreading of the faith, it will seem extraordinary not that it should have taken the passing of centuries for Christianity to become one of the vital forces in politics, but rather that the ideal of life for which Christianity stood should have succeeded in sustaining the great institution of the Papacy.

That the Christian faith had this power was due to the deep inspiration of its doctrines ; but that this power, which was spiritual in origin, should have been directed to the building up and maintaining of a great temporal dominion for the Church, was due to the peculiar attitude of mind of the Christians of the Middle Ages. They never questioned their fundamental assumption that Christianity must spread as Rome had spread, and must aim at a dominion no less universal than hers. At the end of the third century A.D. the Roman Emperor regarded the Christian Church as a rebellious sect ; eight centuries later the Supreme Pontiff, whose seat of power was

Rome, humiliated the descendant of the Roman Emperors at Canossa (1077).

The Dark Ages were dark less because they were lamenting the fall of Rome than because they were nourishing the seed of those ideas which were later to shed a new light on civilisation. Remarkable as were their experiments in the field of political organisation, they succeeded rather in preparing the way for future achievement than in establishing institutions which should themselves survive. Even the Papacy itself, which has been called the " greatest institution in history," offered a contribution which was formative rather than actual. For this reason it was doomed to fall and to give way before the forces of the future, which were making not for world domination either by Pope or by Emperor, but for the triumph of national freedom. The Papacy triumphed, indeed, over the Empire at Canossa, and still dominated the world so late as the early thirteenth century, but its political pre-eminence was short-lived, and it is significant that it was over-come not by the Empire, but by the newly found nationality of France.

The period, then, from the sack of Rome to the fifteenth century, when first the Renaissance and then the Reformation gave a more decisively modern aspect to political thought, covers the story of the growth to power of the institution of the Papacy and of its rapid fall. The Papacy reached the zenith of its influence under Innocent III (Pope 1198–1216), but the ambitious schemes of Innocent IV (Pope 1243–1254) sealed its doom as a political power. He ruined the Empire, hoping that in its fall the Papacy would gain a larger measure of temporal power. In fact, the Empire dragged down the Papacy with it, and both alike were exposed to the growing power of France. The Papacy had arisen to stand for an ideal—the Christian ideal of individual life, which was to replace the Roman ideal of organised comfort and prosperity. So long as it was true to this ideal it dominated men's lives ; but when it forsook its spiritual purpose to tamper with temporal affairs, the plain man turned away from it and looked elsewhere for the realisation of his ideal. The ideal was the same, but it was no longer expressed in the Papacy. In the Renaissance men looked to art and letters, in the Reformation to a reformed religion, and all the while they were building up nationalities of whose importance only occasional thinkers were as yet conscious, but which were inaugurating a new era. The new theory of the State began to be formulated in the crude doctrines of Machiavelli and of Hobbes, but there is no real gulf which separates Machiavelli from the mediæval thinkers, or Hobbes from Locke and Rousseau. Their doctrines are different, but they all form part of one logical development, which began with the teaching of the New Testament of the value of the individual man.

It is, then, to the mediæval interpretation of the ideal of Christian life rather than to any positive political achievement that we must look if we are to understand the attitude of the Middle Ages to politics. It was natural that so far-reaching an inspiration, derived as it was from revealed religion and providing new and divinely authoritative principles for the guidance of human life, could not be immediately assimilated in the actual behaviour even of individual men, still less in that of peoples. Early steps in political progress, under the influence of an inspiration so lofty, would naturally be slow and faltering ; but while so little positive advance was achieved in the sphere of political practice, a new order was being created in the minds of men. If we are really to understand these centuries, we must look to the writings of their great men, bearing in mind how great an influence the New Testament was exerting on their minds. Indeed, for the early part of this era we have to draw almost entirely on the writings of St. Augustine and the Christian Fathers.

St. Augustine was born in A.D. 354, a little more than half a century before the fall of Rome put an end to the organisation which had dominated men's lives and thoughts for five centuries. It fell to him to explain the catastrophe and to attempt to lay down the principles on which was to rest the whole future of the Church. In him, then, we shall expect to find in broad outline the fundamental ideas of reconstruction from which the more specialised and particular doctrines of the Fathers were subsequently drawn ; and this was indeed the case. His work is not primarily an examination of the nature of political society ; rather it is the frank definition of an ideal. The distinction he draws between the divine and the earthly kingdoms, while it definitely marks off this ideal, involves a certain consideration of practical problems which illustrates the nature of early mediæval political thought. His best known work, *The City of God*, clearly marks the beginning of the new age ; out of the world-wide chaos it proclaims the challenge of the Christian Church. Rome had fallen in the Christian era, and so he had to reply to the charge " Rome has perished in the Christian days." He showed how it is the fate of all earthly states to perish; it is only the Divine State, the City of God, which shall survive. This has its earthly manifestation in the Christian Church, which must, therefore, be conceived as higher than the earthly State.

The attitude of St. Augustine to the problems of slavery, property and government—problems which would naturally arise in a period marked both by the development of feudalism and by the growth of monarchies—turned on the distinction between the natural state of man and his life in society as it actually seemed to be. His conception of the state of Nature is directly based on the Bible story of man before the fall ; God made men free and equal, and both slavery and the subjection of man to man in civil government are the result of the fall. Yet human nature is naturally sociable, says St. Augustine, and even though, as a result of sin, man has submitted to unnatural subjection, he still retains something of his natural equality, for he is fulfilling his destiny of living a social life. This destiny he fulfils by living as a member of a freer communion than the temporal State, that is, as a member of the City of God. Thus for St. Augustine, man, being by nature sinful, must submit to subjection in the temporal State, but outside those limits, and as the necessary complement of the secular life, he is also privileged to live as a free member of the great body of the Christian Church.

Thus the problem of mediæval thought is necessarily the problem of the reconciliation of a dual principle of government. Through the fall the temporal State is necessary and must be maintained ; but through his divine origin and destiny man cannot accept the temporal order as the final end of human life. Though he must through sin be a member of the earthly State and must necessarily subject himself to the duties of such membership, he is also called to be a member of the communion of saints. The problem for St. Augustine and for mediæval thinkers generally was to vindicate the possibility of performing both these duties in a harmonious and peaceful life.

The political theory of the Fathers is so far consistent that they do not shirk the consequences of their view of the State of Nature. Since government, they argue, is a divinely appointed punishment and remedy for sin, the ruler must be regarded as the representative by whose means God establishes His divine institution ; he is the " Vicar of God," to whom is entrusted the task of governing mankind, and he is responsible for the fulfilment of his task to God alone. One at least of the Fathers, St. Isidore, does not hesitate logically to follow up this position by maintaining that a wicked ruler is appointed by God no less than a good one, a wicked ruler being a special punishment for sin. Lest it should be thought that this attitude did not penetrate beyond the printed page, it would be well to notice the singular attitude towards the Emperor Maurice taken up by Pope Gregory the Great (Pope A.D. 590–604), whose action is clearly in accordance with St. Isidore's view, and is further interesting because it is in such striking contrast to the subsequent attitude of the Papacy to the temporal power. The letters of Gregory to the Emperor do not manifest a spirit of cringing submission ; obedience is rendered not through fear, but from principle. He points out to the Emperor that his order in the particular case is contrary to justice and to the interest of the Church, and requests him to withdraw it ; but all the time he assures him of his obedience, since he feels that the command of a divinely instituted ruler must carry more authority than a consideration of what is in itself right or wrong in the particular case.

Gregory represents the extreme view, and carries out in his actions the theory of the Divine Right of the Temporal Sovereign which logically follows from the recognition of the divine institution of government. The consistency of the attitude of the Fathers was, however, modified by their recognition of another principle underlying the authority of the temporal power, a principle which was clearly inconsistent with a complete acceptance of the theory of Divine Right and proved to be the basis of the destruction of that theory. Whole-hearted as was their acceptance of authority as divinely instituted and, therefore, commanding unquestioned obedience, they could not refrain from including justice in their conception of the State. " Justice and beneficence," says St. Ambrose, " are the ratio of the State." Thus there is a justification of authority other than that of divine institution alone. In accepting justice as the " ratio " of the State, and hence as the justification of the authority of its government, the Fathers subjected the king not only to God, but also to the

law. Law was to them the expression of the principle
of justice ; it regulated the actions of men in society
and defined their rights and duties in regard to each
other and to their common superior. Thus the power
of the monarch was in a sense granted with one hand
and taken away with the other, for, though of
divine institution, he was not held to be free to deal
with his subjects as he alone thought fit, since he
was expressly termed king under the law. It was
the law, therefore, which regulated his dealings with
his subjects.

The practical development of this principle is
illustrated in the rise of feudalism. The law which
was prevalent in Europe in the Middle Ages was
feudal in character, and for that reason proved
a constant check on the power of the monarchies.
This law depended for its force more on the personal
relations and loyalty of the orders than on written
statutes. It was largely based on custom, but had
nevertheless developed a certain definiteness in its
attitude to authority. It derived its authority not
merely from the king, but from the counsel of the
wise and from the assent of the community. In the
feudal courts a vassal accused by his lord was tried
by his peers. Thus the vassal was to some extent
legally protected against his feudal lord, while the
king or overlord seldom played any part at all in such
disputes. The king was recognised as having
authority over all the kingdom, but loyalty to him
was only indirect, and was generally felt to be less
strong than the tie which bound the vassal to his
particular lord.

Thus, while the authority of kings and emperors

was regarded as derived from God, it was also held to be subject to, and was in practice constantly checked and limited by, the accepted law and custom of the time ; and it was agreed that the theory of Divine Right was only made reasonable in consideration of the moral obligation of authority to maintain justice as interpreted by that law and custom. The king who failed to recognise this duty ceased to be a king, and became a tyrant. The distinction rested on his relation to the law. The purpose of authority was to maintain justice, and consequently, if a king failed to uphold the law of the land, his subjects could claim to be absolved from their oath of allegiance. So, taking their stand on the law which they maintained to have been violated by the tyrant, advanced thinkers, like John of Salisbury, felt logically entitled to advocate tyrannicide. Clearly the admission of justice into the State had led mediæval thinkers some way from the position of the theory of Divine Right.

But this is to anticipate, for this line of development, proceeding from the view of the Fathers that justice falls within the State, tends to lead us out of the Middle Ages into modern times. It was not until the seventeenth century that the monarch's claim of Divine Right was finally subverted by the assertion of the rights and liberties of subjects under the law. The time was not yet come for the slow but permanent vindication of the sovereignty of the people, which does not decay like monarchy or empire, because it is more than an institution. In the Middle Ages the Divine Right of the Empire was submitted not to the rights of the people, but to the rival

authority of the Papacy. It is again to the doctrines
of St. Augustine that we must turn if we wish to
understand the actual line of political development
which culminated in the usurpation of world-wide
power by the Pope of Rome.

St. Augustine alone recognised the complete incom-
patibility of the two views propounded by the
Fathers. As we have seen, he supported the theory
of Divine Right ; but for that very reason he was
driven to oppose the admission into the State of the
principle of justice. If the authority of the sovereign
be maintained to be granted directly by God, it must
be maintained to be subject to the will of God alone.
He emphasises the sociable nature of man, and thinks
that the organisation of the State rests not on the
principle of justice, but on this element of sociability
alone. Thus for him the State is nothing but a
" harmonious multitude of men," and does not include justice. It was not that he thought there was
no justice in the world, or that it could play no part
in men's lives, but that he conceived of it as outside
the civil order, and so as superior, or rather as
parallel, both to civil society and to its ruler, divinely
instituted though he be.

Here, where he differs from his contemporaries, no
less than where he voices their doctrine, it is St.
Augustine who must be taken to represent the spirit
of the age. He developed a logical view of authority
which became the basis of the theory of the dual
government of Church and State as it was variously
developed in the later Middle Ages. With the conception of justice as outside the civil order there
naturally arose the idea that it might find expression

in another order. So the Church came to be looked upon as the embodiment of justice, and hence as an order which is parallel to and not included within the State. Even St. Ambrose, though he had included justice within the State, recognised that there was another and a higher justice which the Church was empowered to administer, and so that the Church had a universal kingdom and could claim jurisdiction over all Christian men.

Thus, while St. Augustine's view seems to provide a basis for this theory of the dual control of Church and State, each authority having jurisdiction within its own proper sphere, his doctrines also proved to be the inspiration for a new idea of unity which was to dominate the political thought of the Middle Ages. By excluding justice from his State, he prepared the way for the doctrine that justice was not included within the State not because it did not play a part in men's lives, but because it affected them in a way with which the State had no concern. So political thought developed from the tendency to recognise an absolute authority in the monarch, not to any theory of complete State sovereignty, but through a conception of a twofold authority to the recognition of an absolute authority indeed, but that not of a temporal monarch, but of the Pope and the Church.

The new idea of unity was drawn from the Fathers, and from the New Testament before them. The inspiration of Christianity, which had taught men to recognise their natural equality, inevitably led to the idea of a universal kingdom. " God in whom we live and move and have our being," said St. Paul ; and the Middle Ages translated this into the conception of a

kingdom embracing all mankind, whose ruler should
have divinely instituted authority. We have seen
how the teaching of St. Paul that civil government
is a divine institution, and that consequently
obedience to the State is a religious obligation, had
been embodied in the early Christian theory of
Divine Right. Later mediæval thinkers adopted this
doctrine, but with it they combined St. Paul's
complementary conception of the freedom of the
Christian man—a freedom not indeed to live in
anarchy, but to keep his spiritual life separate from
his life in society. So, as the basis of the view which
later developed into the conception of a universal
kingdom as instituted by God under the government
of the Pope, we have two apparently conflicting
ideas : first, the idea of the autonomy of the spiritual
life, and hence of the independence of the spiritual
authority ; and, secondly, that of the divine origin
of political sovereignty.

There was no doubt another reason for the appearance of this conflict. Though faced with the problem
of the place and value of the individual, which had
been raised in so acute a form by the doctrines of
Christianity, the thinkers of the Middle Ages naturally started from the conception of the Unity or
Whole. For them always the whole is before the
part, the One before the Many. Every individual
part of the whole unity is itself both part and whole.
Man is a whole as individual, a part as member of the
universal kingdom. The fact that man is in this
sense a part seemed to imply that the whole of which
he is a part must really be a whole, and not merely
a chance aggregate of units. Thus, since all men

naturally belong to one whole, there must needs be one law and one government—that is to say, the kingdom to which men belong must be a universal kingdom. The recognition that there must be two separate orders, the temporal and the spiritual, only threw further back the question of the ultimate authority—for that there was such an authority the political thinkers of the Middle Ages did not doubt.

The ecclesiastical party naturally found this higher unity in the sovereignty of the spiritual power, and claimed that the Pope " held both swords." The Fathers had been saved from a complete acceptance of Divine Right by the necessity of defending the independence of the Church. For them there was a higher justice with which the State had no concern. Moreover, as we have seen, the monarch was in their view only a monarch so long as he obeyed the principles of divine justice. This justice, they claimed, it was the province of the Church to administer. So by easy stages mediæval thought proceeded from this first qualification of the absolute power of the temporal monarch to regard him as no more than an ecclesiastical office-holder.

The political views of the Fathers have been treated at some length, because it is from them that we can best draw a knowledge of the mediæval ideal of life, and, further, because they not only reflected the spirit of their own time, but provided the basis and the stimulus for the thought of the coming generations.

The ninth century was the time of a great change. The coming of the Barbarians changed the whole political aspect of the world, and the Empire of

Charlemagne, who was crowned by the Pope in the first year of the century, superseded the Empire of the East. This new world had at first no real political philosophy ; it depended for its government on a people who had triumphed through force and not through theory. As the Barbarians settled down to assimilate the civilisation they had conquered and took thought of their government, they turned to the Fathers for inspiration. They followed the Fathers in their view that all men are by nature equal ; they learned that slavery and government were institutions appointed by God to remedy sin, being essentially contrary to the natural state of equality ; they were prepared to grant the necessity of this government of divine origin, but the admission did not prevent them from recognising that unjust and tyrannical use of power must be checked. Thus they conceived of the ruler as bound by, and not as superior to, the laws of the nation. From these principles there can be evolved some theory which may be treated as the basis of their practice.

In the eleventh century the great conflict of Papacy and Empire really began. Already, in the beginning of this century, the two authorities overlapped each other ; the Emperors played a great part in elections to the Papacy, while they recognised that they themselves must be crowned by the Pope. In A.D. 1059 the procedure of papal elections was regularised ; and though the cardinals were now given a primary importance in the election, the Emperor still claimed to retain a definite function. But far more wide-reaching in its influence was the difference of view which arose regarding the appointment of bishops. The famous Investiture Contest, concerning the claim of the temporal authority to invest a bishop with staff and ring, the emblems of his spiritual office, came to a head in 1075, and was not decided until the Settlement of Worms in 1122. Both authorities had been stirred to take a practical interest in this matter by their sense of the need for general reform in Church affairs and by their recognition of a marked increase in the abuse of simony— a system by which clerks had to pay for their abbeys and dioceses, and which was doubly disastrous in that it excluded the poor from serving the Church, and that it caused candidates to rob their churches of anything of value in order to pay for their offices.

From the earliest times the clergy and people had, as a general rule, claimed the right of election to benefices ; actually, no doubt, the temporal sovereign played an influential part in the election, and certainly performed the rite of investing the elected candidate with the emblems of office. In 1075 Gregory VII issued a decree prohibiting all lay investiture. Naturally the Emperor was unwilling to give up his control over the bishops, who were always a powerful force in German politics. Writers were found to advocate the claims of both parties ; those supporting the Emperor were especially urgent in their claim that the bishops' temporalities at least should be held from the prince. The outcome of the whole dispute, which continued with varying intensity for half a century, was that the Emperor Henry V surrendered all claim to " invest " with ring and staff, while the Pope agreed that all German elections should be held in the Emperor's presence,

and, further, that bishops should receive their
" regalia " from him—that is, they should hold their
temporal possessions as his vassals. Thus, while the
Emperor admitted that he had no claim to bestow
spiritual office and authority, he retained a general
control of the elections in his kingdom and was able,
further, to maintain his supremacy over the bishops
by his right, recognised by the Church, to give or to
withhold their feudal possessions.

Thus the revolt against the interference of the
temporal sovereign in the affairs of the Church was
first expressed in the new papal policy with regard
to investiture. But Gregory did not stop at this.
Not content with denying the right of the Emperor
to interfere in papal and in diocesan elections, he
himself crossed from the spiritual to the temporal
sphere, and claimed authority to intervene and over-
ride the authority of secular princes. Even before the
beginning of his struggle with the Emperor, he had
already defined his attitude to Philip of France when
he claimed the power to excommunicate and to
depose kings. It was from this claim that there arose
the conflict of Empire and Papacy which resulted in
the famous scene at Canossa, when the Emperor
Henry IV stood barefoot in the snow awaiting the
Pope's pardon. This humiliation involved the tem-
porary abandonment of the Imperial claims that the
Emperor was appointed by God, and was subject to
the judgment of God alone, and that, with the
bishops, he had the right to judge and depose the
Pope. But this was not the end. In the chaotic
years that ensued Henry set up an anti-Pope, and
Gregory a rival Emperor, who was to acknowledge

himself a vassal of the Papal See. These conflicts only served to distract Europe, and did not permanently benefit either party, though ultimately a working settlement was reached between Henry V and Pope Paschal II (A.D. 1110).

The history of this struggle shows clearly the lengths to which society was driven by its rigidly dualistic conception of authority. The demand for a final unity of government, which was so strongly characteristic of the Middle Ages, raises at any time problems of the greatest difficulty in regard to the rival claims of spiritual and secular life; but for the Middle Ages this problem could only be settled by an agreement between the Papacy and the Empire. Things would have been difficult had every Pope and every Emperor been perfectly good and perfectly wise; but as things were, with the claims of the Pope, however stupid or bad, was bound to stand or fall the ordinary man's claim to spiritual independence, while in the humiliation of the Emperor he saw an attempt to repudiate once and for all the necessary independence of political government. As we have seen, this attitude of mind was, in part, the fatal legacy of the Roman Empire; for the people of the Middle Ages the struggle between the two world empires, the spiritual and the temporal, was the settling of a speculative problem; it never occurred to them that it might be settled in any other way. It never occurred to them that perhaps one of those empires was standing for the guaranteeing of a right which no system of world control can guarantee, but which any such system must in the end subvert; that, in other words, the desire for spiritual independence requires for its satisfaction not the independence of a spiritual autocracy from the temporal power, but the independence of the individual free man to live his own spiritual life. They thought that the spreading of the Christian faith and the living of the free spiritual life could only be secured by the organisation of a spiritual world Empire. So the useless battle had to be fought to a finish, for the Middle Ages saw no other way of settling the question.

In the middle of the twelfth century John of Salisbury published his *Policriticus*, a book which may fairly be taken to represent the growing tendency to support the supremacy of the spiritual power. John was an Englishman and a bishop. Described as the "most learned gentleman of his day," he divided his time between his library and the society of eminent and cultivated Churchmen. He was on intimate terms with Adrian IV, and did not scruple to speak his mind on the faults of the Papacy, even going so far as to repeat to him the criticism that "the Holy Father himself is burdensome and scarcely to be borne." His book, the *Policriticus*, is typical of the man ; it was dedicated to Becket, and, nevertheless, contains much frank advice on the needs of the Church. His general position, however, depends on the doctrine of the supremacy of the spiritual power. As the soul rules the body, he says, so the heads of religion in the State are set over the whole body politic. The first duty of the ruler is to reverence and worship God ; and as the head of the body is to the soul, so the prince or head of the State must be to the priesthood. In John of Salisbury, too, we find the doctrine of the two swords, which plays so prominent a part in mediæval writings. Two swords, one spiritual and one temporal, were given by God to St. Peter, who, through the hands of the Pope, gives the temporal sword to the prince or ruler, who is thus instituted by, and can be judged by, the spiritual power.

It is not difficult to trace the development from this position to that of the scholastic philosophers, or schoolmen, as they were called from the part they played in mediæval education. Their theory of a temporal monarchy embodied in the papal power was a natural fruit of mediæval thought, and affords an explanation both of what had gone before and also of the reaction against papal supremacy which followed in the attempts of Dante and Pierre Dubois to vindicate the building up of a temporal world empire independent of and supreme over the spiritual power.

John of Salisbury had compared the world to the human organism, and had concluded that the prince must be ruled by the priesthood as the head is governed by the soul. The schoolmen took their stand on the doctrine of the value of the individual, a solid foundation which would carry far more weight than could such an artificial comparison. St. Thomas Aquinas (1227–1274), the greatest of the scholastic philosophers, seems to give expression to all that was best in the thought of the Middle Ages ; and though he stood at the threshold of a different age, he was more truly representative of their spirit than any thinker since St. Augustine. St. Augustine, too, had been only half a product of the Middle Ages, for he had combined with the new Christianity something of

the spirit of the ancients, leaving the succeeding
generations to absorb what he had preserved. So,
also, St. Thomas Aquinas, for all his genuinely
mediæval characteristics, was not altogether alien to
the spirit of the Renaissance and the Reformation.
While the fourteenth century was the time of the
birth and chaotic growth of new forces and new ideas,
the thirteenth supplied a breathing space in which
men were able to look back on the past and take stock
of its achievement without being exercised as to the
immediate future. So St. Thomas Aquinas looked
back on the achievement of the past and saw before
his eyes the established power of the papal monarchy.
Recognising its existence as a fact, he tried to justify
it by emphasising the part it played in the development of the individual.

The fundamental doctrine of St. Thomas and of the
schoolmen was that the individual alone has ultimate
value, and that therefore the State comes into being
and must continue to exist for the good of the
individual life of its members. Side by side with this
view of the value of the individual, there was in him
a strong sense of the prevailing mediæval passion for
unity ; he asserts that God is the ultimate authority,
since in Him all things are one. This leads him into
a somewhat paradoxical position in that he advocates, on the one hand, democracy, and on the other
the absolute authority of the Pope. The government, he says, of any State is with God, Who alone
can direct all things for the sake of each man's
virtuous life, which is the end of the State. From
God the authority passes to the whole group of men
which is the State, and they dispose it in the hands

of one, or of a few, or of the many ; whatever the form of government, it is the people who are sovereign under God.

Thus in temporal matters Aquinas recognises the right of the individual to a share in directing the government of his State in the interests of the good life of himself and of his fellow citizens. In spiritual matters, on the other hand, the individual must, he says, submit himself wholly to God ; for man belongs to two orders, seeking in the one a natural and in the other a supernatural end. While in the order of nature God, as it were, delegates to man the authority to regulate the State in the interests of the good life, in the spiritual order He submits man to the supreme jurisdiction of the Pope, who is His representative on earth. So, from his doctrine of the value of the individual, St. Thomas seems to be assigning a divine origin to democracy ; but in the end this apparently liberal doctrine only proves in his hands a weapon for the repudiation of any empire which might rival the Papacy, and so binds even more closely the supremacy, or rather the almost irresponsible autocracy, of the spiritual power.

The same principles, however, which led St. Thomas Aquinas and others of the ecclesiastical party to establish the Papacy as the dominating force in politics were capable of supporting a different construction. It is from the same source, namely the emphasis on the value of the individual, that Dante, in his *De Monarchia* (published between 1310 and 1313), derived the opposite conception of a temporal world-empire. Dante thought that the individual's primary need was peace, because it was peace that

enabled the human mind to perform what he conceived its proper function to be, that is to say, to use
its discursive intellect. It seemed to him, therefore,
that the ideal constitution of society would be that
which most surely guaranteed that peace. His
characteristically mediæval mind concluded that it
was unity which was necessary to this end, and that,
therefore, mankind must be united into a single
State. All human beings had, he argued, a common
end, since it was peace they all desired, and the
peace of each could only be secured by the harmony
of all. Thus we are led to Dante's view of the
necessity of a universal kingdom under the supreme
and all-controlling power of a monarch. In spite of
his advocacy of such a constitution, Dante seems to
have confined his reverence to the ideal monarch, and
showed scant respect for such mortal men as had, in
fact, held such a position in the actual order of
things ; he certainly does not allot to kings the
places of honour in his *Divine Comedy.* Yet,
although his ideal monarch is not a picture of an
actual ruler, it is difficult not to feel that his
ideal world-empire admits a particular application
prophetically to Italy and historically to Rome. In
his great work, the *Divine Comedy,* Virgil was the
companion of his wanderings through Hell and
Purgatory, and it is not unlikely that he would
enliven the more tedious parts of the journey with
discourses on " the splendour that was Rome." At
any rate, it seems to have been through Virgil that
Dante turned to Rome for inspiration and found in
the Roman Empire an example of the possibility of
a world-peace. There he found a firm rock on the

memory of which he could lean amid those wars of the
Middle Ages which were reaching their height of confusion and intensity in his time—for him the Roman
Empire stood for peace, and it is not surprising that
it should have been taken as a model for a possible
reconstruction of Europe. So Dante turns to the
temporal power for salvation ; he makes light of the
arguments for papal supremacy and relegates the
functions of the High Pontiff to the supernatural
sphere. This, then, was Dante's view of the relation
of the two powers : the Empire exists to help man
to attain his earthly end in a universal peace, while
the Pope leads him to eternal life.

It was world-peace, too, that was the ostensible
purpose in the theory of Pierre Dubois (1250–1312),
the champion of the principle of nationality newly
discovered in the monarchy of France. Dante's *De
Monarchia* was the last attempt to advocate a
world-empire on the old model. In the fourteenth
century the nationalist spirit rose to prominence, and
for a brief space the two ideals existed side by side.
This century was an age of transition, and Pierre
Dubois was typical of the age. His political theory
is a strange complex of the mediæval and of the
modern ; for, while retaining the old ideal of unity,
and hence of a world-empire, he rejects both the
Papal and the Imperial interpretations of its meaning,
and substitutes the conception of a national king.
That peace which had been the end of the theories
both of St. Thomas Aquinas and of Dante was, in
his view, to be secured by the domination of France.
The reasons he alleges for the necessity of French
supremacy are unconvincing to the modern mind ;

although most nationalist adventures in pursuit of empire do, in fact, start from the same insecure basis, namely, a national or personal conviction that the particular people or the particular king are supremely destined by God to rule the world. Pierre Dubois, like Dante, attributed the origin of the State to the common needs of mankind, and especially to their need for peace. Again, like Dante, he thought that this peace was to be secured by a universal kingdom ; but he fuses a modern conception with this mediæval doctrine when he sees in the national kingdom of France the future mistress of Europe.

The rise of French supremacy involved the destruction of the temporal power of the Pope. The Empire had gone under in the long struggle with the Church, and the time was now come for the Church herself to yield to a new enemy. The subjection of the Papacy to France was remarkably swift. In A.D. 1300 Boniface VIII had challenged the authority of all secular governments by his proud boast, " I am Cæsar, I am Emperor." In 1305 the French king had secured the appointment of a French Pope, and established him at Avignon ; and the Papacy was exiled from Rome. So Pierre Dubois was speaking with a knowledge of the facts when he inveighed against the temporal power of the Papacy ; it had stood in the way of the aggression of France, and the French king had swept it from his path ; and Pierre approved the act.

The extreme swing of the pendulum away from the doctrine of ecclesiastical supremacy came with Marsilius of Padua, whose famous work, the *Defensor Pacis*, appeared in 1324. It was only ten years later than the *De Monarchia*, and deals largely with the same problems, but the difference in the solutions suggested represents more than a decade's growth, for it amounts to a complete change of attitude. Marsilius' condemnation of the Church, indeed, has little to distinguish it from the attacks of Dante and of Pierre Dubois, and it was this point which chiefly attracted the attention of contemporaries. But his substitution of the sovereignty of the peoples of the world for that of monarchy stamps him as a political thinker of a new type. Again we meet the view that the origin of political society lies in a general recognition of common needs ; again we find security emphasised as pre-eminent among these needs ; but from the first a new feature is present in the insistence that " this security is but the means to man's higher well-being." Marsilius thinks in terms not of right and wrong, but of needs which must be satisfied as a preliminary means to this ethical end when he asserts that laws are necessary to regulate men who are by nature perverse. So, in order that men may live together peaceably and be enabled to pursue their well-being, they must be under a government which will assign to each his function. Thus in the theory of Marsilius, as in the practice of Imperial Rome, we find some return to the doctrine of Plato, that that state is just where every man has a task to do, and does it well. For Marsilius, however, there is one class of men in society, namely the priests, who seem to perform no necessary function, except in so far as they may help to police mankind by the dread they inspire of the punishments of hell. In spite of his claim to rest his view on the Scriptures, he was blinded to the spiritual function of the priests by his hatred of their temporal power. He was convinced that the Church was the most dangerous enemy of that security for whose sake men formed societies and submitted to government; and so he was led to try to establish in his argument points which would represent the Church as insignificant in comparison with the State. He particularly emphasised the view that the clergy have no title to property, and asserted that the Pope's view that " the clergy were the Church " rested on an error, since the Church was in reality the " universitas fidelium," or " whole congregation of Christians."

Thus Marsilius appears as a forerunner of Luther in his opposition to the Papacy. In this respect, however, he was but voicing the general feeling of his time. His real contribution to political theory lay less in his condemnation of the power of the Church than in a constructive plan for the organisation of society. His revival of the Platonic conception, together with his assertion of the sovereignty of the people, show that he was preparing the way for the development of a non-mediæval view of society. And, indeed, when Marsilius wrote, the Middle Ages were already giving way to the new era. During the fourteenth century men passed from a mediæval to a modern world, and the change was marked by a revival in the arts and by the Reformation in religion. The humiliation of the Papacy before France and the Avignon captivity finally opened the eyes of men to behold what had long been a fact— the inadequacy of the Papacy alone to supply them with an ideal which should wholly guide and inspire their lives. So men turned away from the Papacy and looked first to art and letters, and later to a reformed religion, for the expression of their ideal of life. Neither Renaissance nor Reformation of itself supplied men's needs, but it was only through them that an advance was possible towards a conception of society which might, with better reason, dominate men's minds in the future, as the Papacy had dominated them in the Middle Ages.

CHAPTER IV

THE REFORMATION : HOBBES AND THE DIVINE RIGHT OF KINGS

WITH Machiavelli (1469–1527) we are at the beginning of a new age. In the past centuries society had set itself an ideal of life which it had been unable to fulfil ; and now at last both the ideal and the partial achievement which had been secured were alike disregarded by a new doctrine, which claimed a hearing because it was based on fact. Machiavelli sought to construct his view on an analysis of the actual practice of the princes of his time. The regulations of society had long ceased to attempt even to approximate to the ideal which Christianity had set before Governments, and the separation between ethics and politics, which had been emphasised by Aristotle but repudiated by the Christian element in mediæval thought, was now restored. It fell to Machiavelli to restore it in theory as the princes of Italy had restored it in practice.

His real position in writing his great work, *The Prince*, is open to various interpretations. Rousseau describes it as the " Republican's manual " ; but whether or no Machiavelli was a democrat at heart and meant to propound, not a defence, but a " reductio ad absurdum," of the principle of monarchy, it cannot be denied that in his writings he stands

forth as the wholehearted advocate of the most
atrocious tyranny. His choice of a hero is significant.
After relating the deeds by which Cæsar Borgia rose
to a position of pre-eminence in Italy, he concludes :

"Taking all his actions together I can find no fault
with him ; nay it seems to me reasonable to put him
forward as I have done as a pattern for all such as rise
to power by good fortune and the help of others. For
with his great spirit and high aims he could not act
otherwise than he did, and nothing but the shortness of
his father's life and his own illness prevented the success
of his designs." [1]

If it be remembered that Cæsar Borgia was the son
of Pope Alexander VI., and used his father's position
as spiritual head of Christendom to further designs
for his own temporal aggrandisement, it becomes
clear that justice and the rights of peoples did not
enter into Machiavelli's calculations. The adventurer
who overran Italy to carve out a principality for
himself in defiance of the wishes both of the people
and of their legitimate rulers may be an example of
the success of unscrupulous recklessness, but he can
hardly be held up as a model to princes who would
live at peace with their subjects and with the world.

The importance of Machiavelli for us is that he
gives a cool, dispassionate judgment on the politics
of the Middle Ages. It was his professed intention,
as it was no doubt temperamentally a delight to
him, "to call a spade a spade." It seemed to him
better, as he said, "to follow the real truth of
things than an imaginary view of them." He had

[1] Machiavelli, *The Prince*, Chap. vii.

as data for his analysis a long experience of political
life which in width and variety was second to that
of no man of his age. It was the cool judgment of
this man that in politics success comes to the unjust
rather than to the just ;

" the manner in which we live and that in which we
ought to live are things so wide asunder that he who
quits the one to betake himself to the other is more likely
to destroy than to save himself, since anyone who would
act up to a perfect standard of goodness in everything
must be ruined among so many who are not good.   It is
essential, therefore, for a prince who wishes to maintain
his position to have learned how to be other than good,
and to use or not use goodness as necessity requires." [1]

Now it must be remembered that this was written
by a man who was for many years secretary to the
Council in the Republic of Florence ; who during
that period executed many and various missions for
his native state and was always credited with an
intense patriotism. Though he lived in an unscrupulous and self-seeking age, there is no evidence that
the confidence which the Republic of Florence
reposed in him was ever withdrawn, or ever even
wavered. Machiavelli was in all his political life an
intense patriot, and he was in constant contact with
other Florentine patriots. If we believe, as surely
we must, that the doctrines of *The Prince* really
represent his considered view, our conclusion must
be that he thought not that there are in mankind no
finer feelings than base self-seeking, but rather that
as a ruler and a patriot no man can afford to show

[1] Machiavelli, *The Prince*, Chap. xv.

finer feelings—indeed, he has no right to show them.
Only so can a ruler maintain the position of his
state as against other states ; foul dealing may well
be his duty as a ruler. " It is essential," he says—
and we may be allowed to repeat the quotation—
" for a prince who wishes to maintain his position to
have learned how to be other than good, and to use
or not use goodness as necessity requires." Any
one who reads the history of the Middle Ages in the
light of this doctrine will easily understand that a
patriotic thinker might well cry out in some such
words as these : " Let a prince abandon high-
sounding ideals of religious duty, and let him do
something which will really improve the condition of
his people or increase the majesty of his state ; if he
does this it will easily be forgiven him that the
means he uses are in themselves difficult to justify."
Read in this way, Machiavelli is seen to have made
an honest attempt to offer a solution of the political
problem, and, given the conditions under which the
world was then living, his solution would no doubt
appear the only practicable one.

This position could not, however, long remain un-
challenged. It might be true that a prince could only
secure the prosperity and dignity of his kingdom by
obeying the principles of Machiavelli, and it might
well be true that any honest, well-meaning prince
who had at heart the interests of his people must
recognise, if he ever thought for himself, that he must
adopt such principles in his action. But Machiavelli's
book, by painting the society of the Renaissance in
its true colours, showed the world that, however little
an individual prince might be to blame, there must

be something wrong with the world system which made such things necessary. So it was possible for the simple judgments of a plain moralist, such as Luther, to cut like a knife through the elaborate conclusions of Machiavelli's closely reasoned argument. A system so rotten at the core must be swept away. Luther could not wait to be taught that authority must sometimes depart from the dictates of ordinary morality if political society is to be maintained. The Machiavellian prince might argue that, though it might be wrong for the ruler to do this particular thing, it would be a greater wrong for him to risk the fall of the authority and the kingdom for which he stood in order to satisfy his own personal conscience ; against such ingenious ratiocination Luther stood like a rock—his position did not admit of being moved by argument. " Here I stand, I can no other, so help me God." This simple challenge to the whole world system of civil and ecclesiastical authority was able to stir emotions which were to move Europe more profoundly than could any intellectual conviction. Perhaps we may be allowed to pause for a moment on our way and enjoy the significant drama in more detail.

In 1517 A.D., Tetsel appeared in Wittenberg to sell indulgences to replenish the coffers of the Papal See. By an extension of the interpretation of the command given to St. Peter—" I will give unto thee the keys of Hell and of Death "—the Pope had assumed the authority to forgive sins : this came to mean that the agents of the Pope sold at a price certificates proclaiming the forgiveness through the Holy Father of particular specified sins, and this Tetsel and his crew came to do in Germany, in 1517. On October 31st of that year Luther nailed to the door of the University Church in Wittenberg his *Ninety-five Theses against Indulgences*. Yet Luther did not fully realise till four years later that his position would inevitably involve him in rebellion against the Church.

At last, however, he stood out firmly for the principle of "the Freedom of the Christian man." Religious life, he thought, concerns only a man and his Maker : the Christian can admit of no earthly authority in spiritual things. He saw that a man always is and must always be responsible for his every action, no matter at whose command he does it : just as a man must choose for himself in matters where authority does not decide for him, so also must he choose for himself when authority does so decide—he has to choose whether or not to obey authority, and nothing can relieve him of the responsibility of that choice. This was a new way of looking at authority, and it opened a new era in political thought.

Gradually, as the doctrines of the Reformation spread, men came to see more and more clearly that they need not, indeed that they ought not, blindly to accept the form of authority under which they were placed, whether it were secular or spiritual. So in political theory men at last began to ask the question, " Ought we or ought we not to obey the State ? " And naturally enough and rightly enough they tried to answer this question by first solving the question, " Why, in fact, do we obey the State ? " This is the question that faced both Hobbes and

Rousseau. Hobbes facing the constitution of England of his time, asked himself the question, " Ought I as a free Englishman to obey this sovereign ? " and the answer he found in his heart was " Yes, I ought." He then put to himself the question, " How can it be that I as a free man ought to obey a despot ? " and his political theory represents his attempt to find the answer—the attempt to explain how, in fact, free men do come to obey, and rightly to obey, despotic monarchs.

Thomas Hobbes of Malmesbury (1588–1679), from whom English political philosophy may be said to take its rise, wrote his first political work, *The Elements of Law Natural and Politic*, in 1640. In this book, which was only circulated privately in manuscript, Hobbes sketched out the position which he later fully elaborated in his great work, *The Leviathan* (1651). He seems to have united in himself a bold independence of opinion with a remarkable timidity of character ; and in view of the latter quality the genuine originality of his thought proved a source of great inconvenience to him, since none of the political parties of his time seem to have seen its implications sufficiently clearly to be able to define their position with regard to it. Thus on the appearance of *The Elements of Law Natural and Politic*, Hobbes fled to the Continent through fear of Parliament, while after the Restoration the charge was brought against him that his book was " writ in defence of Oliver's title." The truth is that Hobbes honestly worked out his theory from first principles, with the result that it coincided with the doctrine neither of the Royalists nor of the Parliamentarians. As we shall see, Hobbes really cared little whether sovereignty rested with king or with Parliament (though, no doubt, he thought monarchy was the simplest form of government), provided only that the principle be admitted that, with whomsoever it rests, sovereignty must remain indivisible and inalienable.

Hobbes starts his political inquiry with an analysis of human nature. He maintains that the actions of men always are, and are bound to be, based on wants and desires. Those wants and desires are not in themselves either good or bad ; they are just facts, part of the fundamental nature of human life and human activity. Without some want or desire to move a man in the first instance, there would be no such thing as action ; and however it comes to be that actions may be in themselves good or bad, certainly no such distinction can be made among these elemental wants and desires. " The desires and passions of men," he says, " are in themselves no sin ; no more are their actions, till they know a law which forbids them." [1]

This view of human nature, which seems to contain within it much which is essentially sound, Hobbes presents in a very misleading way. He appears sometimes to have thought that once upon a time there really were men living in this state of simply having desires and satisfying them, and with no inclination or necessity to think of anything but their own desires ; living, as it were, " from hand to mouth," and having in their minds no consciousness which might affect their action, but merely the

[1] Hobbes, *Leviathan*, Ch. xiii.

appetite of the moment. In this state every man is thought of as acting just as it pleases him and never finding in his experience any reason for not doing anything which amuses him. This state of man Hobbes calls the State of Nature. It is like the conception of man before the Fall—man who knows not good from evil because he lives in a world where there is no evil, and therefore no good.

For Hobbes, however, the absence of a consciousness of good and evil did not mean that man was happy. All men, as he saw, are equally entitled to satisfy their own desires without feeling the necessity of any constraint upon such satisfaction. Men are, moreover, endowed in equal measure with " strength, prudence and wisdom " ; and " from this equality of ability there ariseth equality of hope in the attaining of our ends." [1] This leads to that enmity between man and man which necessarily makes of the State of Nature a State of War. The picture which Hobbes draws of this State of War is black indeed.

" Whatsoever is consequent," he says, " to a time of war, where every man is enemy to every man, the same is consequent to the time wherein men live without other security than what their own strength and their own invention shall furnish them withal. In such a condition there is no place for industry because the fruit thereof is uncertain, and consequently no culture of the earth, no navigation nor use of the commodities that may be imported by sea, no commodious buildings, no instruments of moving and removing such things as require much force, no knowledge of the face of the earth ; no

[1] Hobbes, *Leviathan*, Ch. xiii.

account of time, no arts, no letters, no society, and which is worst of all, continual fear and danger of violent death, and the life of man solitary, poor, nasty, brutish and short." [1]

This, according to Hobbes, is the natural state of mankind. From this wretched lot it is the task of civil society to rescue men once and for all; and it is because civil society is all the time preserving them from this State of Nature, into which they would always be slipping back if it were not for that "mortal god," the State, that the sovereign can rightly claim from all subjects an absolute obedience. If we are to understand Hobbes' theory of the State, we must realise that he was always emphasising the power of this great force in human nature which is ever tending towards disorder and the State of Nature, and whose fell influence can only be checked by an all-powerful, absolutely sovereign State organisation.

To say that this disorderly force was regarded as being the element of wickedness in man would be to misrepresent Hobbes and to neglect the most valuable element in his doctrine. No doubt he sometimes speaks as if he thought the problem was caused by the wickedness of man; perhaps he sometimes thought himself that the selfish evil-doer was the most potent enemy of law and order; and he points out that in maintaining such a view he would only be logically carrying out the views of the ordinary householder, who locks his chests every night and carries arms when he goes abroad. But the careful reader of *The Leviathan* will detect that there is

[1] Hobbes, *Leviathan*, Ch. xiii.

something deeper in Hobbes' view than this. Hobbes does not merely say that in the absence of a constraining power men act from selfish desire ; he adds that there is no reason why they should not do so : in the absence of a legislating and coercive authority there is no justice and no injustice. Hobbes seems, in fact, to be maintaining that an analysis of human nature shows that there is, quite apart from the badness of mankind, a real problem for civil society to solve—the problem, that is to say, of making it possible for man to live a rational and orderly life, distinguishable from that of the beasts. He thinks that without civil society such a life would be impossible, however good men were by nature ; the arrangement of life so that every man can pursue his own purposes without making it impossible for other men to pursue theirs demands more than goodness and benevolence in the individual ; it demands the institution of civil government, that is to say, it demands the co-operation of man with man.

If we are to be in a position to estimate the truth of this conclusion, we must first examine more closely the analysis of human nature. Hobbes concluded, as we saw, that there can be no morality and no consciousness of obligation prior to the existence of law and government. Until there is a law, all actions are equally good and right ; whether a man kills a sheep for his supper or kills his brother in a moment of anger, there is no distinction of goodness or badness between the actions, since there is as yet no law which forbids either action. Clearly there is a certain truth in this view.

It is no doubt difficult now for us to make up our minds on so abstract a point as this, since we know that man never did and never could live in any such State of Nature, free from and unaware of any principles constraining his action. After all, every man is necessarily born into a family, and we know that even in the most primitive societies the family fits into its place in some larger group, and that these groups are ruled by rigid customs, which are as readily obeyed as are the laws in a more fully-developed society. But though the question is thus an abstract one, we may not altogether avoid it in this way; and we may perhaps throw light upon the difficulty by comparing the Bible account of primitive man with that of Hobbes. In the Bible version it may no doubt be urged that Cain was not conscious of doing anything wrong in raising his hand to strike his brother, but at any rate, when he realised that he had killed him, he was ashamed. He seems to have recognised that he had done wrong without waiting to be told. There seems, then, to have been in his consciousness something which was not a desire or a passion; it was not merely that Cain wanted to have his brother alive again, not merely that he thought it stupid to have killed him. He knew that it was wrong, and his defence, " Am I my brother's keeper ? " showed a very definitive understanding of moral principles.

This account seems to be based upon a truer psychology than that underlying Hobbes' view. Clearly, if he were right, it would never have occurred to any man to think of himself as his brother's keeper. Hobbes saw, indeed, that, as soon as men come to

live together, reason becomes operative in their
actions as well as the desire of the moment ; but he
assumes that man is the same creature throughout,
and that the appearance of reason makes no difference—that he still acts from desire, while his reason
just serves to make him more competent to satisfy
his desire. In this Hobbes seems to have been wrong.
The truth surely is that, when man comes to think,
he necessarily feels ashamed or proud of himself ; if
once he reflects on his action, he must think of it as
either good or bad.

It would seem, then, that in so far as Hobbes
maintained that there could be no recognition of
right and wrong and no consciousness of obligation
independently of the existence of civil government
it is impossible to agree with him. But although we
may urge that the individual may do good actions
independently of society, we must yet admit that
this capacity for moral action can never in itself
ensure that men may live together in peace and
security ; the institution of civil society is still
required for this purpose, and, as Hobbes saw, it
represents the only means of bringing about such law
and order. The desires of different people are no
more likely to fit naturally into a harmony when
those desires are good than when those desires are
bad ; and, as history shows, there have been no more
inveterate quarrels than such as arise between men
whose conceptions of duty differ. To prove that man
has a conscience and that his conscience can affect
his action is not to prove that men will live in
harmony. Such harmony can only be produced by
some form of co-operation under a civil government.

The incalculability of the life of mankind in so far
as it is not controlled by authority depends not on
the wickedness of man, but on the fact that he is
free. Yet man can only use his freedom or obey his
conscience under a system where the conditions of
action are to some extent calculable. As Hobbes
urges, in the State of Nature the best and wisest of
men is necessarily helpless, since he knows that
obedience to the higher principle within him can
bring about nothing but his own destruction ; and
no man can really will his own destruction nor feel
it to be his duty to do so. Thus it seems to be true
that, without some form of civil government,
morality is impossible.

Thus whenever we notice—as we are bound to do
again and again as we proceed—Hobbes' apparently
excessive fear of the tendency of mankind to lapse
into the State of Nature, we must not mislead our-
selves by thinking that this is simply due to an over
estimate of the wickedness of mankind ; it is, in fact,
to be attributed in a much larger degree to Hobbes'
recognition that, if once the organised control of
human affairs is allowed to slacken, the clashing of
individual wills grows steadily and irrevocably, and
produces results which could not have been foreseen—
and the whole society is drawn irresistibly into an
anarchic disorder which it cannot control. Though
every man appears to be acting freely, yet the
resultant of all these free actions is the appearance
of certain determined tendencies before which the
individual is powerless. It is to deal with this
problem that civil society came into being, as men
gradually came to realise that by co-operation they

could achieve a mastery over this natural anarchy. In this sense there is no possibility of free action and no possibility of just action except under a civil society.

The founding of society by means of a contract involves, indeed, the recognition not only that there was a condition of man prior to society, but also that in that condition men enjoyed something which they relinquished on entering the society. Thus Hobbes recognises that even in the primitive natural state there are, in some sense, " laws of nature," and that man has corresponding rights. But there is no feeling of obligation connected with these laws, and this " right of nature," the gift with which man is endowed at birth, is simply " the liberty each man hath to preserve his own life." [1]   If self-preservation is the sole natural end of man, then all the regulations of conduct which he employs to secure that end are, as Hobbes says, " general rules found out by reason, by which a man is forbidden to do that which is destructive of life." [1]

The first of these rules or " laws of nature " is to " seek peace and follow it," for it is through peace that men can best preserve their lives. This desire for peace impels men to unite according to Hobbes' second law, which lays down that men shall relinquish their right to all things " which, being retained, hinder the peace of mankind." Here, again, it is quite clear that this rule is regarded as in no sense a moral law, for Hobbes makes it quite clear that, on his view, society is formed by a voluntary act. Man

[1] Hobbes, *Leviathan*, Ch. xiv.

gives up deliberately his natural right to use his own judgment in the exercise of his power to preserve his own life in order to secure some advantage to himself. This advantage lies in the fact that others likewise give up their rights, and that the sovereign to whom all alike have submitted will guarantee their security. Finally, there is another law of nature to which Hobbes appeals in order to emphasise the binding nature of the covenant—the law that " men perform their covenants made." This law, again, is a " general rule found out by reason," without which it is impossible to gain that " peace and security of life " which is regarded as man's highest good.

Man is thus induced to make the social contract by obedience to these " laws of nature " or " rules of reason." But Hobbes hastens to assure us that we must not suppose that men consent in the observation of justice and in the maintenance of the covenant without a common power to keep them in awe ; for then " there neither would be any need to be any civil government or commonwealth at all, because there would be peace without subjection." [1] A condition of peace for mankind can only be secured by the institution of a supreme coercive power—by the absolute and forcible subjection of the many to the sovereign, to whom they have transferred their rights. Since the existence of society depended on the maintenance of this supreme, irresistible power in the hands of the sovereign, it was clear that sovereignty must be regarded as inalienable, for it was essential

---

[1] Hobbes, *Leviathan,* Ch. xvii.

to civil government that there should be no power in the State strong enough to gainsay the sovereign ; therefore, sovereignty could never be transferred.

For this reason, Hobbes was led to maintain that the covenant was final and irrevocable. The only way, he says, for men to erect such a common power as may be able to defend them is to confer all their power and strength upon one man or one assembly of men. This is—

" more than consent or concord ; it is a real unity of them all in one and the same person . . . who by this authority given him by every particular man in the commonwealth hath the use of so much power and strength conferred on him that by terror thereof he is able to perform the wills of them all to peace at home and mutual aid against their enemies abroad." [1]

From this institution of a commonwealth are derived " all those rights and faculties of him on whom sovereignty is conferred by the people assembled " ; and when once this conferring of power is agreed to, it is final and cannot be revoked. If the people seek to remove the sovereignty from him whom they had endowed with it, they thereby return to the State of Nature, and lose all the benefits which society had been instituted to guarantee. In attacking the sovereign they attack the society, for sovereignty was granted once and for all, and not given by covenant with the sovereign, nor, as Hobbes says, " on condition." The covenant that was made at the institution of society was one between subject and subject ; between subject and sovereign there could

[1] Hobbes, *Leviathan*, Ch. xvii.

be no covenant, since the sovereign must rely for his authority upon force, and not on any covenant, "which, being but words and breath, has no force to oblige, contain or constrain but what it has from the public sword, that is, from the united hands of that man or assembly of men that hath the sovereignty." [1]

Thus the sovereign has absolute power and absolute authority, and can, as far as his subjects are concerned, use his power for whatever end he thinks fit, and will therein commit no injustice. For all men are held to be the author of that which the sovereign does, and cannot, therefore, blame him or seek to punish him or put him to death. There is, besides, annexed to the sovereignty an absolute right, and indeed a duty, to maintain undisputed authority over all his subjects ; he has the power to judge them, to call them out to war, to choose his ministers, and to reward and punish. "These," says Hobbes, "are the rights which make the essence of sovereignty, and are the marks whereby a man may discern in what man the sovereign power resideth, for these are incommunicable and inseparable." [2] So the sovereign can do his subjects no wrong ; he is responsible for his actions to God alone. "He that doth anything by authority of another," Hobbes says, "doth therein no injury to him by whose authority he acteth." And again, "It is true that they that have sovereign power may commit iniquity, but not injustice or injury in the proper signification." [2]

Hobbes, then, while he made the upholders of

---

[1] Hobbes, *Leviathan*, Ch. xviii.   [2] *Ibid.*

Divine Right his enemies by his curious view of the
secular origin of political authority and his refusal to
regard the lawful claims of the monarch as relevant,
held a theory which was in other respects identical
with the Royalist doctrine. He may be said to have
upheld a doctrine of the "Divine Right of any
Government which can, in fact, command obedience." While he always inclined toward monarchy
as the most convenient and simplest form of government, he was, in fact, attacking neither King nor
Parliament, but rather the division of power between
the two ; such division of the sovereign power he
saw to be incompatible with the maintenance of civil
society. Sovereignty, he urged, must be with either
the one or the other, and where it lies there it must
remain ; only so can man preserve himself from the
State of Nature which is the state of war. There is
something almost divine in the nature of this great
Leviathan, the State, and of its governor ; Hobbes
describes him in words taken from the Book of Job[1]:
"There is nothing on earth to be compared with him.
He is made so as not to be afraid. He seeth every
high thing below him ; and is king of all the children
of pride." In fleeing from the anarchy of the State
of Nature, in which the individual finds himself helpless, man finds himself inevitably cast into the powerful arms of Leviathan, that mortal God before whom
he is equally powerless. These are the only alterna-
tives for man—the state of war or Leviathan ; between these man can choose—or rather between these
mankind once did choose, for there was only one
possible choice.

[1] Hobbes, *Leviathan*, Ch. xxviii.

It is perhaps difficult at first sight to think oneself into the position in which Hobbes found himself. We must remember that he regarded organised society as created from beings who have no consciousness of anything but simple desire.   Although man thus acts from selfish desire alone, he has come, as Hobbes saw, to live his life in a fully-developed society, within which there is found law, reverence for law, and a recognition of obligation to obey the law.   All this seems to have arisen out of nothing, since it is natural to mankind to live at enmity and in a state of war.   Organisation is contrary to Nature, and yet it is clearly essential to human life and human happiness.   Since, then, civil society has fortunately arisen among us, we ought to be thankful that it is so and to be diligent in preserving it at all costs.   For, thought Hobbes, if we do anything which may bring into disrepute and destroy this wonderful fabric of order and peace, what have we to put in its stead ?   We have nothing ;   we must just fall back into the State of Nature, which is the state of war.   If his analysis of human nature had taught him that it was natural to men to co-operate for the universal maintenance of justice and in pursuit of a common end, Hobbes would have taken a different view of the State.   But as it was, for him law and reverence for law were not at all based on any fundamental recognition of what is right and what is wrong ;   they were simply ordinances of prudence arrived at by a kind of composition or truce, to which men were finally driven by their experience of the state of war.   If the present system were abolished, there would be no underlying principle of justice or consciousness of common purpose to which appeal could be made in advocating and establishing a new order.

This view is a common enough one in politics. "Somehow," it is said, "out of chaos man has evolved by his own reason a system, a *modus vivendi*, in which he has come to believe and which he can understand. We do not understand how it came to be ; we cannot see how order ever started out of disorder. Let us, then, at all costs preserve this ground so hardly won ; for if we went back at all toward disorder, how should we ever again emerge ? Laws are necessary ; let us then keep those laws which we have, and which are by long custom accepted and obeyed. If it is to our interest to have a new law to-day, it may be equally so to have a different one to-morrow ; and laws such as these could have no more authoritative standing than that of any single decision of any one of us, and so we should be back again in the State of Nature. It is the permanence and remoteness of the laws which makes people obey them. Since, then, it is necessary to human happiness that there should be fixed laws which all will obey, let us be thankful that we have such a system of law, and let us maintain things as they are lest worse befall us."

This was the position in which Hobbes found himself ; the demand, inspired by the Reformation, that the institution of authority should be justified before the judgment of the individual man found thinkers of his time unprepared, and Hobbes could do little more than express his surprise that civil society should have emerged at all. He saw clearly that under the existing order men had a real respect for the law, and while he saw the benefits which this respect for law ensured, he failed to discover its origin. Hobbes had rejected the possibility that this respect was due not so much to the actual laws themselves as to those underlying principles of justice which the laws were regarded as embodying, albeit imperfectly; for he thought such principles did not exist. For him that which commanded obedience was the actual existing law, as written in the statutes, and the actual person exercising sovereignty. He thought that the only possible check on action from selfish desire was that certain rules should be definitely laid down and enforced as the regulations of society. These would at first be obeyed only under the influence of force, though later under the influence of that awe inspired by time and custom; but in any case obedience could only be guaranteed by keeping them fixed and unchanging as they stood.

A doctrine similar to this has inspired the political creed of many men in all ages; it is indeed an intelligible one. For any man it is a grave responsibility to wake again the forces which a successful civil government has laid to rest; to rouse the passions of a people, nobler and baser alike, and to endeavour to pilot them through anarchy to a higher self-realisation, to a form of constitution which sacrifices less that is valuable in the struggle for order and organisation. For Hobbes it was worse than this. For him there could be no such progress through anarchy; for him all that mankind had won from chaos and disorder was and must be contained in the actual existing form of government. If that were lost, all was lost. On Hobbes' view, the only standing that a law can have is that it is accepted and that it is obeyed; therefore the law as accepted and obeyed must be maintained, for if it is destroyed nothing is left, nothing at all. All this wonderful fabric of order and peace which has been built up with such toil and such suffering through all the generations of our ancestors—all this would be gone, leaving not a wrack behind!

So Hobbes was driven to maintain the sanctity of the person of the sovereign and the inalienability of his power. He had shut himself off at the outset from the view that respect for law and the possibility of society rest on something more profound than a written law or even a particular constitution; for at the bottom of the human soul he found nothing but selfish desire, and in the world around him he saw nothing but things for man to desire and things for him to detest. He saw that with the appearance on earth of government and law there appeared also reverence and law-abiding orderliness, new attitudes of the human soul which would make possible a new and happier life—the life of a community with peace within its walls. But Hobbes did not see that this arose because man represented to himself the law as aiming at a higher, nobler, truer justice than was expressed in the mere words of the law. He thought that the respect must be for the law as formulated, since the appearance of the law caused the appearance of the respect. So he thought that to tamper with one jot or tittle of the law was to destroy that respect, and with it civil society, and so to lose eternally the ground mankind had hardly gained in its long struggle upward from the State of Nature and the State of War.

The conception of sovereignty involved in this view is closely akin to that of the theory of Divine Right, with the exception that Hobbes does not insist that sovereignty must reside in one man, or that the choice of the man rests with God. The history of the development of society from the original contract shows, if we are to believe Hobbes, that it is only by resigning all power, once and for all, into the hands of a sovereign that social life becomes possible. If it is the sovereign and the sovereign alone who makes possible a life nobler than the state of war of every man against every man, then there is assuredly something divine in his office—a view which is made all the more credible by the inalienability of his power, which endows him with a permanence akin to that of the eternal laws of the universe. If you believe with Hobbes that there was a time prior to society when men lived a life little different from that of the beasts, then you may well agree that he who rescues them from that state and places them within reach of a more human existence is entitled to their eternal gratitude and obedience. It is not even surprising that men should think of such a one, or of his established successor, as appointed by God, and as such all the more irremovable, if they recognise the nature of their condition prior to his coming and appreciate the change he has made possible.

Objections to this position have followed two different lines; for it can be maintained both that society emerged by a far different process from that described by Hobbes, and that the state in which the subjects of such a sovereign are forced to live is worse even than the state of war. If the king be held to be endowed with an absolute authority to treat his subjects as he thinks fit—and we have seen that Hobbes insists on this, and removes from the subjects even the right of complaint—then it is possible that the position of his individual subjects may be worse, even from a material point of view, than it was prior to society. For then each man relied on his own arm for his defence, and did not trust in a sovereign whose treachery might at any moment rob him of liberty or of life. In the State of Nature none would be brought to such a pass as have been the most faithful servants of princes. Strafford, when he died for having upheld his king in the exercise of what he himself believed to be a right divine, could not complain of his fate, but he could at least warn others against it by his dying words : " Put not your trust in princes."

If a king is " good " and governs in the real interests of his people, as would, for example, Bolingbroke's " Patriot King," then, no doubt, his subjects do derive great benefit from his rule, and both their material and moral welfare are to a great extent secured under the law and order which he maintains ; but there are few who would honestly claim that the monarch has a " right divine to govern wrong," and that God, as it were, appointed a bad king to chastise his people. If it is in the power of the subjects to rid themselves of him, they need not think that they are offending God by so doing, since the king has been untrue to his trust in persecuting his subjects. So far Bolingbroke would agree, but Hobbes does not seem fairly to face the issue.

Bolingbroke, no less than Hobbes, failed to realise that the principle involved in the absolute sovereignty of the monarch was in itself open to fatal objections, even apart from the goodness or badness of particular kings. However much of his authority the sovereign may appear to resign in allowing his subjects to come and go in apparent liberty, so long as he is and is recognised to be all-powerful and to stand above law and justice, so long the citizens must be prepared at any moment to submit to his arbitrary pleasure, and must recognise that their life and liberty depend on his word. Such a condition may appear to be hardly preferable to anarchy. Moreover, since history bears witness to the growth of States where order and efficiency have been combined with individual liberty, it is impossible to maintain that such sacrifice of liberty is inevitable in the interests of law and order. If it were inevitable, the life made possible by society would not be nobler than life in the State of Nature. Even such as would be prepared to agree that Hobbes' conclusion follows from his premises would scruple to agree with him that "peace and security of life" is the ultimate end of man on earth. There have been men in all ages who have weighed their lives as nothing against some principle of conduct, and have gladly gone to the stake in defence of a name. Whether or no martyrs are to be considered freaks of nature, to be left out of account in a serious consideration of political society, there is a spirit akin to theirs at work in all communities. It may be that the only possible standard for the calculation of men's actions is one of self-interest, but if this be so, the greater part of action cannot be calculated at all.

In neglecting this Hobbes neglected a vital part of man's nature, and was unable to see the whole truth about political society. Both he and the advocates of the Divine Right of Kings missed the importance of the individual man not only as entitled to rights, but as an actual force in politics. When Hobbes denied the existence in man of any moral instinct, he may have seemed to be doing no more than expressing an opinion ; but in truth he was shutting his eyes to a fact.

It is idle to discuss the rights of the sovereign and to ignore not only the rights, but the powers, of the subject. A king may claim his title by right divine, but his subjects may deny it to him on no other authority than that of their individual conscience. Action in opposition to the sovereign, which to Hobbes could not be rational at all, since it could not spring from self-interest, proves itself a very real force when it brings the established authority tumbling like a house of cards about the heads of the advocates of Divine Right.

CHAPTER V

ROUSSEAU : THE GENERAL WILL

HOBBES had tried to construct a conception of human society from an analysis of the nature of individual man. He had failed not because his method was a wrong one, but because his analysis was incomplete. Rousseau, who pursued the same method, was led to an entirely different view by his ability to grasp truths which lay beyond the field of Hobbes' vision. Like Hobbes, he started from an examination of human nature, but he saw in man more than a mere creature of desires and passions.

Both writers recognised that it must in the end be a free act of choice by which any man remains a member of or obeys the commands of society. Both realised that, therefore, society must be such that a man can choose to obey it ; and both to some extent realised—though this point is more prominent in Rousseau than in Hobbes—that it must be such that a man would be right in choosing to obey it.

Hobbes attempted to explain in principle the individual's obedience to society on a basis of the purely rational pursuit of selfish interest ; Rousseau attributes it not to such a rational calculation, but to the moral judgments of the individual conscience.

Instead of concluding with Hobbes that obedience must be rendered to the existent authority for the sake of the security which it guarantees, he insists that, in spite of the danger to security, man is bound to resist any authority and any institution which seems to him incompatible with man's individual liberty. He sees that it is man's nature to treat wrong as wrong, and to be prepared to risk even his life to set it right. It is significant that Kant acknowledged his gratitude to Rousseau for opening his eyes to the " moral dignity of the individual."

Hobbes' theory had, however, been already modified by subsequent writers before Rousseau swept it away by repudiating the conception of man as a purely selfish being. Hobbes had maintained that the end of civil society was security of life and property, and since it was only by the maintenance of order that such security could be attained, it followed that political government, when once established, must be for ever inviolable. On his view, no malfeasance on the part of the sovereign could entitle men to disregard his authority. Such disobedience would for Hobbes have meant the dissolution of the society, since he drew no distinction between the agreement to form a civil society and the agreement within that society to set up some particular government. Locke (1632–1704) emphasised this distinction both as a justification of the Revolution of 1688 and in the interests of a more liberal doctrine of sovereignty, which his views regarding that Revolution had led him to seek. This modification of Hobbes' view of the irrevocability of the contract can admit

the finality of the covenant by which the society was
formed, while denying that any particular government need command any but a transitory obedience.
It is the fact of the existence of the society which
makes possible the life of its members, while the
government of the moment does no more than
organise the means of securing those rights which the
society exists to guarantee.   Therefore, as soon as the
members of that society think that the laws and
commands of the particular government are contrary
to the interests of the community as a whole, it is
possible for them, as Locke saw, to change the
government without destroying the continuity of the
civil society itself.   For since it was the civil society,
and not the particular government, which was
thought to be established by the social contract, a
change of government might be effected without any
violation of the covenant.   This, as Locke would
maintain, is what actually happened in the Revolution of 1688.   It would be absurd to suggest that on
the abdication of James II the English State ceased
to exist, and that a new civil society was formed
whose sovereignty resided in the persons of William
and Mary and of the Lords and Commons of
England.   What did happen was simply that the
people who formed the English State changed their
form of government, and the sovereignty which had
formerly resided in James was transferred to William
and Mary in Parliament.

The conclusion from this doctrine was immediate,
that, since the people have the right to change their
government, and even their form of government,
the real sovereignty resides all the time not in any

government, but in the people themselves. So the
people of England transferred the supreme authority
from James to William and Mary in Parliament ; and
so a century later the American people transferred
it from the government at Westminster to a constitution and a government of their own. The
American Revolution was in logical accordance with
Locke's doctrine, and the new constitution it set up
was founded on the principle of popular sovereignty
which had characterised his writings. It becomes
clear, indeed, from an examination of the language
of the Declaration of Independence that the founders
of the American State were profoundly influenced by
Locke's thought, and even by his terminology. In
arranging the details, however, of the form and
organisation of the actual constitution they adopted,
they turned elsewhere for inspiration. This they
found in the writings of Montesquieu.

Montesquieu (1689–1755) was a scholar rather than
a reformer. He was primarily interested in the
investigation of the actual facts of political life. This
interest led him to develop a new political theory as
the result of a critical analysis of actual constitutions.
He did not claim to be primarily a champion of the
cause of freedom, but his study of politics led him to
conclude, first, that the people were ultimately
sovereign, and, secondly, that it was to the interest
of society that this should be so. These clear-cut
views, set out in an arid style untinged by any
sentimentalism, seem to have appealed to the
Puritanism in the Americans of 1779 ; at any rate,
most of Montesquieu's conclusions are to be found
reflected in their constitution.

of the period and its account of the different Socialist organisations."

WEBB, S. and B. *Industrial Democracy*. Longmans, 2 vols. [1897.] A detailed account of the structure and function of Trade Unionism.

WEBB, S. and B. *A History of Trade Unionism*. Longmans. This covers much the same ground, but is more detailed historically, and carries the story up to date. [Revised Edition, 1920.]

WEBB, S. and B. *The Consumers' Co-operative Movement*. Longmans.

BEER, M. *History of British Socialism*, with an Introduction by R. H. Tawney. Bell, 2 vols. This book is " a study of political thought upon the group of problems created by the rise of Capitalist agriculture and Capitalist industry." The general reader will probably find all that he wants in this book.

Among detailed and original essays to work out Modern Socialist Theory, the following books seem to be of chief importance :—

WEBB, S. and B. *A Constitution for the Socialist Commonwealth of Great Britain*. Longmans. The authors first point out a number of objections to the Capitalist system, and estimate the good already achieved by various democratic associations under existing circumstances. They then explain that " what the Socialist aims at is the substitution for this Dictatorship of the Capitalist of government of the people by the people and for the people in all the industries and services by which the people live." Then follows a practical attempt to work out a detailed system of democratic control on the principles of State Socialism.

COLE, G. D. H. *Self-Government in Industry*. Bell.

COLE, G. D. H. *Social Theory*. Methuen.

Mr. Cole thinks that " the State, however important, is and can be no more than the greatest and most

permanent association or institution in society, and its
claim even to any such position will have to be carefully
considered." He works out more or less in detail a
system of democratic control on Guild Socialist principles, suggesting that sovereignty in the State should
be a " Co-Sovereignty " between a Parliament of Consumers and a Parliament of Producers.

HOBHOUSE, L. T. *Elements of Social Justice.* Allen and
Unwin. This book contains an interesting criticism of
Mr. Cole's theory. The author does not agree with
Mr. Cole that " a study of the State in its relation to
the individual cannot penetrate to the heart of the
question of man's place in society." He considers that
" Politics must be subordinate to Ethics " (p. 15, note).
As its title suggests, the book as a whole is rather
theoretical and general than practical and particular.

It is also necessary to add the following books, which
give an account of some practical attempts to deal with
modern political problems. The most interesting practical
developments of recent years seem to be those connected
with the League of Nations, the Constitution of the British
Empire, Fascism and the Soviet System.

PERCY, LORD EUSTACE. *The Responsibilities of the League.*
Hodder and Stoughton.

JOHNSTON, G. A. *International Social Progress.* Allen and
Unwin.

POR, ODON. *Fascism.* Labour Publishing Co.

FERRERO. *Four Years of Fascism,* translated by F. W.
Dickes. P. S. King.

POSTGATE, R. W. *Bolshevik Theory.* Grant Richards.

Finally, it will be worth while to include a number of more
general books which do not readily fall under any heading :—

HETHERINGTON, H. J. W., and MUIRHEAD, J. H. *Social
Purpose.* Allen and Unwin. These lectures discuss the
difference between man as an individual and man as a
member of Society.

LOWES DICKINSON, G. *A Modern Symposium*. Dent. A discussion designed to bring out the different attitudes to Politics current in modern England.

WALLAS, GRAHAM. *Human Nature in Politics*. Constable. An analysis of the ways in which the working of political institutions is in practice affected by the actual facts of human nature as revealed by psychological inquiry.

LOWELL, A. L. *Public Opinion and Popular Government*. Longmans. An attempt to estimate how far and in what way Government is and can be controlled by public opinion.

FOLLETT, M. P. *The New State*. Longmans. An interesting book, which is appreciated and criticised by Bosanquet in his Preface to the second edition of " The Philosophical Theory of the State." Miss Follett repudiates " the ballot box and the rule of numbers." What is wanted, she says, is a " new spirit in politics." " It is not only that we must invent machinery to get a social will expressed ; we must invent machinery to get a social will created." Group organisation will do this : " The group organisation movement means the substitution of intention for accident, of organised purpose for scattered desire. It rests on the solid assumption that this is a man-made, not a machine-made, world." " We are asking for group organisation in order to leap at once from the region of theory, of which Americans are so fond, to a practical scheme of living."

ZIMMERN, A. E. *Nationality and Government*. Chatto and Windus. A collection of lectures and articles on the future of the British Commonwealth, and on the attitude likely to be adopted in the future to the principle of Nationality.

INDEX

193